ʦ

understand

your

teen

A PRACTICAL GUIDE TO
THE PSYCHOLOGY OF
PARENTING TEENAGERS

KAIREN CULLEN

Published in the UK
in 2019 by Icon Books Ltd,
Omnibus Business Centre,
39–41 North Road,
London N7 9DP
email: info@iconbooks.com
www.iconbooks.com

Sold in the UK, Europe and Asia
by Faber & Faber Ltd,
Bloomsbury House,
74–77 Great Russell Street,
London WC1B 3DA
or their agents

Distributed in the UK,
Europe and Asia
by Grantham Book Services,
Trent Road, Grantham NG31 7XQ

Distributed in South Africa
by Jonathan Ball,
Office B4, The District,
41 Sir Lowry Road,
Woodstock 7925

Distributed in India
by Penguin Books India,
7th Floor, Infinity Tower –
C, DLF Cyber City,
Gurgaon 122002, Haryana

Distributed in Australia and
New Zealand
by Allen & Unwin Pty Ltd,
PO Box 8500,
83 Alexander Street,
Crows Nest,
NSW 2065

Distributed in Canada
by Publishers Group Canada,
76 Stafford Street, Unit 300,
Toronto,
Ontario M6J 2S1

Distributed in the USA
by Publishers Group West,
1700 Fourth Street,
Berkeley, CA 94710

ISBN: 978-178578-450-7

About the author

Kairen Cullen is a writer, a chartered educational psychologist and a parent of four adult children. She trained as an educational psychologist and achieved a PhD at the Institute of Education, University of London. She has worked for several decades with individual children, young people and adults to help them achieve educational and personal success. She has also done a lot of work with groups, organizations and the press and media. She has now reached the point in her career where she has decided to use her extensive experience for writing, consultation and media-related work and no longer offers the individual assessment services through which, in the past, she helped with a tremendous variety of learning and behavioural issues. You can read about the wide range of topics and publications to which Kairen has contributed and her other work on her website http://drkairencullen.com

In recent years Kairen has also taken up creative writing, drawing upon her experiences to create fiction, and she is working hard to develop this new venture.

Author's note

In my assessment practice I have helped people to clarify their issues, questions and the changes they wanted to bring about. I did this through a process of finding out as much as possible about the factors and influences contributing to their situations in order to provide professional advice. I used 'positive psychology' with a firm commitment to the humanistic psychology principles of acceptance, congruence and empathy. I also drew upon a number of applied psychology approaches including cognitive behaviour therapy, art therapy, family therapy, solution-focused brief therapy and personal construct psychology. I continue to use these approaches, my research skills and psychological theory in my writing, other professional activities and in my life generally as I have always believed it to be essential to 'walk the talk' and to provide services which I would be happy for myself or a member of my own family to receive. Where at all possible I have referenced the source of research drawn upon in my writing but in instances where these may have been overlooked I offer my apologies.

Contents

Section 1:
Introduction to the psychology of parenting teenagers

1. About this book

This is a book for anyone who has anything to do with teenagers and cares about their well-being, development and learning: actual parents of teenagers, parents with younger children who in time will become teenagers and also the many other adults in teenagers' lives, including professionals who may find the text helpful as an aid to thinking in their practice. It offers an original, practical and theoretically informed way of thinking about, understanding and actually living with and being involved with teenagers.

I am writing from the perspective of an experienced professional educational psychologist, who at various times has specialized in 'behaviour', which as most people know is shorthand for 'difficult behaviour', and very frequently that of young people in the teenage years. I am also drawing upon my life experience as the parent of four adult children who, of course, were once teenagers with a fair few of the blessings and challenges that teenagers bestow on their parents and the world in general.

The focus of my book is largely on what is considered to be 'normal' teenage behaviour, i.e. not upon the range of behaviours associated with clinical disorder and what is sometimes termed 'abnormal psychology'. However, I will touch upon the signs and symptoms that can be evident when these latter terms may apply, what to do in those situations and who might be able to help. It is important for me to emphasize that where a young person's everyday behaviour, learning and/or development is causing concern and is significantly different to that of the majority of other children in their age group, then adults involved with such young people should seek advice and possibly the direct input of appropriately qualified professionals. The family's GP and/or an involved education professional are generally good access points for getting this help.

This book is strewn with case studies, which of necessity are fictional but, as for nearly all fiction, are drawn from lived experience. Practical tips and exercises accompany the different challenges of teenagers, often within the case studies in order to better understand the ideas presented. You may decide to try some of them with your own teenagers and if so you need to select activities which you are confident are appropriate, supportive and always undertaken with the young person's well-being and best interests in mind. If, for whatever reason, it is not feasible to do the exercise with an actual teenager, I suggest that you draw upon memories of being a teenager yourself and use your remembered and/or imagined younger self.

The approaches that I have developed in my applied practice are underpinned by educational psychology literature and psychological theory in general and I will summarize and refer to these where appropriate. The last part of this introductory section, Chapters 4 and 5 focus very specifically on many of the theories that I draw upon. I outline the blend of research and theory that is being used and aim to clarify and explain this so that readers gain a practical understanding that will help them in their relationships with teenagers. I also provide references for further and more in-depth reading for those who wish to pursue their explorations of the subject more.

This book follows my first book in the Practical Guides series published by Icon Books, *A Practical Guide to Child Psychology*, first published in 2011 and now available in its second edition. This book builds upon many of the ideas in my first book and you may find it helpful to read this also.

The key ideas

How you use this book will of course depend upon your particular situation, and the nature of your involvement with teenagers. This is not a book of instruction and it does not claim to have all the answers, or to be able to 'prescribe' exactly what you should do. However, it will help you in your thinking, and as we all know, whether or not we are professional psychologists, little true learning, solution-finding or even behaviour as a whole changes unless an individual's thinking is open to new ideas. This, itself, is a key idea that runs through every chapter, so even if you find some of the ideas and approaches not immediately appealing, **try to stay open-minded** because there is every chance that you can blend some aspects with other ideas and approaches.

This leads nicely to another key idea: the need to **cultivate creativity** in your interactions with teenagers.

My mum is always reading books or listening to people on the radio on how to deal with me and I can see where she's coming from from a mile off. It doesn't work because it's not real and it wasn't her idea.

Fourteen year old

In many ways teenagers today are more informed and worldlier than ever before. New technology is partly responsible but I also think, from my experiences with so many teenagers over more than three decades, that their reasoning and questioning is more sophisticated than ever before. This is a testament to both our education system and to parents and carers and is a reflection of the world we live in. This is why it is important to be as original, authentic and relevant to the particular young person and situation as possible. If you aren't, they are sure to find you out. As one colleague said to me:

Teenagers can sometimes seem like an unstoppable force because they generally have one overriding project into which they channel their energies and emotions and that is themselves.

Child psychiatrist

This quote illustrates my third key idea, which is that **teenagers are generally very self-focused**, and think about themselves a lot. If you want to test this out turn to any popular fiction or television representation, or if you kept a diary at this age yourself, read this and the inward gaze of most teenagers is clear.

Perhaps when I am famous and my diary is discovered people will understand the torment of being a 13¾ year old undiscovered intellectual.

> *The Secret Diary of Adrian Mole,*
> *Aged 13¾ (1982) by Sue Townsend*

So on to the next idea: **If you want to find an answer ask a question**.

Drawing on the generally self-focused nature of teenagers, it makes sense that if you are trying to help, support and guide them, then talking with and asking them about their issues, challenges, wishes etc. is a good idea and is often likely to be the starting point and at least a *part* of the solution to any problem.

Please note the italics above as I want to highlight the substantial contributions that parents and adults offer to the teenagers in their lives. With this in mind here are some of the things that adults can offer teenagers:

- Life experience and a sense of perspective
- Love
- Encouragement
- Affirmation and endorsement
- Role models, based upon the 'do as I do' style rather than the 'do as I say' style
- Information
- Resources

THINK ABOUT IT

Make your own additions to this list on the previous page.

I hinted at the fifth key idea in the above bullet point about 'do as I do', and it is to **be congruent in terms of your own behaviour, including what you say**. If you don't immediately have an answer or a solution, it is best to be honest about this, but also realistically positive. For example: 'I don't know at the moment but I think I know how to find out.' I am confident that this book will help you at such times.

It is also key to enforce the idea that **teenagers need to experience the world in order to learn**. Because the world they are growing up in is different to the one that their parents grew up in, this can make their sometimes impetuous, risky and experimental behaviours a source of concern and worry. When people are anxious they generally seek to be in or have more control and as the average teenager pushes on a daily basis to have more control of their actions and choices this can and often does lead to conflict. It does not help that the general portrayal of teenagers in popular media emphasizes this negative aspect, so I am deliberately re-framing this issue as that of the teenager doing what they can to learn what they need to know and do in order to grow up into independent, functional adults. I also suggest that you as a parent of, or someone living on a daily basis with, a teenager, view the fact that they are often their most difficult with you because they are secure enough to risk and engage in the conflict and know you can manage the negativity and the sometimes painful emotions. Although you may not like their behaviour, your love for them is always there.

Work as a professional psychologist entails many years of study, daily ongoing reading and research, supervised professional practice and a conscious striving to always work with objectivity, neutrality and scientific rigour, so I am not downplaying any of this when I say that my next key idea is that **we are all psychologists in our own lives**. The reason for this, I believe, is because although psychology is a complex and vast subject, most of what psychological theory and research can offer to people in their everyday lives is eminently practical and useable. Once you have developed a greater understanding of the psychological theories relevant to your situation you will be in a better position to use this in reducing and resolving problems.

Another key idea is that although there are undoubtedly generalizations to be made about the teenage years, **every teenager is different and unique**. Each teenager has their own developmental path, their own unique, innate characteristics and each experience different living situations and conditions. Human beings are complex, dynamic and many-faceted entities who live in an ever-changing world and the view that teenagers embody these characteristics particularly obviously is a common one. The adults with whom they are involved have to reconcile their own, usually quite vivid and often difficult memories of being teenagers with the demands and responsibilities of their own adult lives and be supportive and wise in relation to their young people. However, it must also be recognized that **every parent is unique and different** and will have their own unique situations, personal and material resources and histories. My clinical and personal experience tells me that the only way to achieve this is through the following final key idea: **parents need to be engaged in continuous, everyday problem-solving and solution-finding**. This necessitates energy, realistic optimism, stamina and confidence. I am hoping that in the pages to come you will find some fresh, accessible and practical ideas that you can use in your involvement with the unique teenagers with whom you are involved.

 Ten key ideas within this book about interacting with teenagers:

1. Try to stay open-minded
2. Cultivate creativity
3. Teenagers are generally very self-focused
4. If you want to find an answer ask a question
5. Be congruent in terms of your own behaviour, including what you say

6. Teenagers need to experience the world in order to learn
7. We are all psychologists in our own lives
8. Every teenager is different and unique
9. Every parent is unique and different
10. Parents need to be engaged in continuous, everyday problem-solving and solution-finding.

---

2. The teenage years

Historical and social context

In the Western world, until the 20th century, the phase of life that we now know as the teenage years was relatively new. It was not acknowledged as an explicit aspect of society embedded in everyday culture the way it is now across most of the world. The distinction between children and adults was less demarcated and child labour was commonplace until the law changed, very gradually, to prohibit such practices. A new legislative framework was put in place over time, mandating minimum age requirements for sexual consent, marriage, school attendance and work and then at a later stage for voting, driving and alcohol consumption. The time that children spent in compulsory education was being extended, school populations were becoming more diverse and integrated, i.e. in terms of socioeconomic, ethnic and racial characteristics, and the expectation that young people in their mid-teens should be married was changing.

The common behaviours and underlying attitudes of young people, for example in relation to drinking, smoking and dancing, began to be evident from the 1920s onwards, although the terms 'teenager', 'teen' and 'teenage' were not commonly adopted across the world until the mid-20th century. Contributory factors included the popularization of the car, the development of public transport, improved communication systems, the civil rights movement, women's emancipation, the development of female contraception, a culture of dating independent of direct parental supervision and an enlarged freedom and range of personal choice regarding leisure time and would-be boy and girl friends. This was extended by much larger and better-resourced schools serving wider geographical areas and a more mobile population affecting and changing family and community structures. All of these factors, inextricably linked with two world wars and a subsequent mushrooming consumer economy and advertising industry, contributed to the popular culture within which the teenage ethic of fun and freedom, reflected in their expectations, attitudes and behaviour, was evident and apparently increasing for subsequent generations of teenagers. These changing values typified by the 'average teenager' prompted accusations of materialism and self-gratification of the young and, in fact, can still be voiced by older people even today. It is also true that the teenage years have been and still are very commonly seen as synonymous with a problematic age – a time of rebellion, questioning, anti-social behaviours, challenging lifestyles and experimentation. However, another more positive view often amplified by popular media and the arts is that teenagers are frequently and increasingly trendsetters, with their own distinctive and new fashions, music and film and exciting technology-related culture.

As would be expected, the scholarly study and societal preoccupation and fascination with teenagers developed alongside all of the above and continues today. For example, although not originally written with teenagers specifically in mind, the founding father of psychodynamic theory Sigmund Freud's assertion that the libido was one of the most powerful and natural of human needs has been viewed by some as contributing to an endorsement and legitimization of teenagers' wish to explore and test society's mores and limits. If parents search online for writings and advice about teenagers they will have no shortage of material from which to select.

Global patterns

Being a parent, no matter where in the world you and your family live, brings many challenges and blessings. Most parents will relate to this quotation written over 400 years ago:

> *The joys of parents are secret, and so are their griefs and fears.*
>
> Francis Bacon, philosopher, 1561–1626

The job of being a parent is like no other and yet all of the following points are universal:

- It continues throughout life
- There is no job specification or contract
- There is no salary or expense account
- It involves huge responsibility
- It requires the investment of large amounts of emotional and physical energy and material resources

- Everyone, including relatives, friends, society at large and the children themselves, especially adolescents, will have views on how well you are doing
- Every parent has to create their own style of parenting to suit their particular children and family situation.

With the availability of so much information and advice about parenting through new technology, different parenting styles have gained currency across the globe and selecting the right one for you and your teenager can be daunting, not least because it is easy to feel criticized by others when you don't get things exactly right. In addition, cultural, social, religious, economic and political factors, which vary both within and between different countries, all play a part in the particular challenges that parents and their teenagers face. For example, in the West at this time mental health problems, obesity, drugs and alcohol are just a few of the highly publicized and debated issues that parents and teenagers face. In other parts of the world, conflict and war, the migration of large groups of people, poverty and famine all have a huge impact upon children's and teenagers' development and well-being, family structures and family and community life.

It is undoubtable that some parents' challenges are much greater than others but there is no rating scale of difficulty with which to measure these, and different parents in even the worst conditions vary in how resilient, capable and proactive they can be in relation to caring for their children and enabling them to grow into independent and functional adults.

Media – influences and issues

Fifty years ago this section would have been much harder to fill. Now we live in a world that is so influenced by and reflective of 'the media' that it is hard to select and summarize the most important aspects and do the subject justice. If this is a topic with which you wish to engage in more depth, then I recommend a book by Strasburger et al. (2009), listed in the reference section.

You may find some of the ideas in Chapter 16, which focuses on helping with concerns about young people's lifestyle choices and their behaviour surrounding these, useful.

The key aspects of teenagers' lives influenced by media include:

- Lifestyle choices and choices about how to spend leisure time
- Consumer behaviour
- Learning about the world, i.e. social, political, physical, factual ideas
- Learning from teacher-directed curriculum-related material
- Online socialization
- Relationships and social behaviour, including sexual behaviour

- Dysfunctional and anti-social human behaviour, e.g. violence, conflict, war, self-harm, suicide
- Mental health issues
- Body image and physical health
- Culture
- Spirituality.

 Think about yourself as a teenager and pick a couple of your favourite TV programmes or films from that time. What did you learn from them?

Working with involved adults and within the psychology profession, the concerns that I often hear regarding teenagers and media are:

- Young people are spending an unhealthy amount of time and energy using phones, the internet, video games etc. at the expense of other more social and physical activities

- Young people are overly influenced by the images and behaviour depicted in the media and this can result in them copying anti-social and/or dysfunctional aspects in their own lifestyle choices and taking unwise risks

- Adults feel unable to monitor and control the online content their young people are watching

- Teenagers can make themselves vulnerable to sexually, political and/or commercial predatory and exploitative individuals, groups and organizations

- Teenagers' use of new media can be harmful to their mental health and well-being

- Teenagers' use of new media can be harmful to their relationships, especially with family and older people who are relatively uninformed and uninvolved with the online worlds being accessed.

The issues outlined above are commonly expressed by journalists and producers who ask for my professional comment and I have noticed that recently some other angles have been introduced. These include the issue that increasingly younger children are using new technology, that parents are using new technology as pacifiers/entertainment rather than actually interacting with their children and that young people are rejecting traditional reading and viewing material – books and television – in favour of what they can access online. There is definitely a climate of moral panic and even fear being expressed by adults and this therefore, ironically, adds more to the attraction of new media for teenagers, as it's another opportunity for rebellion and area for questioning.

When thinking about how to manage teenagers' seemingly excessive use of new media, an either/or approach, which involves banning or imposing strict curfews, can seem to be the easiest and clearest method. However, in my experience, this subject calls for more of an 'and/both' approach that allows the young person some choice and control in setting limits to their screen time. More than any other aspect of contemporary society, new media is almost certain to stay and to develop as it offers such an array of opportunities for information, entertainment and communication. Younger people in particular are embracing it enthusiastically so the care, guidance and support adults can give teenagers in using it in a way that supports their best interests and general well-being are needed more than ever. The relationships between parents and teenagers have developed over time, and the shared personal histories and sheer emotional investment and commitment mean that most young people know that the guidance parents give can be trusted and is not driven by commercial interests.

The law and teenagers

The age of majority: the age that children become adults, and are therefore responsible for their actions and decisions rather than the responsibility of their parents, varies across the world from as young as fifteen years to 21 years. However, in many countries young people who marry, regardless of chronological age, gain legally recognized adult status. This age of majority is not necessarily a reflection of the individual's physical and mental maturity but it does set the limits in relation to their freedoms and actions.

In the UK, from the age of sixteen to the age of 21, certain entitlements are made explicit in the law. These relate to a long list, including:

- Relationship choices, including those of a sexual nature
- Accommodation – buying and renting property and moving out of the family home to live independently
- Marriage
- Medical treatment and choices – registering with a doctor, consent for dental, medical or surgical treatment
- Study – entering higher education, gaining access to educational records
- Work, for example joining the armed services, and earning the minimum wage
- Benefits
- Voting
- Jury service
- Standing for parliament, local councils or as mayor
- Opening a bank account
- Making a will
- Pawning goods
- Gaining access to birth certificate if adopted
- Buying and consuming tobacco and alcohol
- The watching of select viewing material
- Betting – playing the lottery or football pools
- Driving, or becoming a driving instructor
- Adoption.

Most young people are very interested to learn about their legal rights and the specific ages at which different prohibitions and choices are available to them. Ask them to read the list above and next to each item decide at which of the following ages these are applicable: sixteen, seventeen, eighteen or 21 years.

I recommend you then have look together at the information available on this Mumsnet web page: https://www.mumsnet.com/teenagers/legal-rights-at-16

This page relates to sixteen year olds but there are equivalent lists for seventeen, eighteen and 21 year olds.

Criminal responsibility

It must be noted that the age of criminal responsibility is another matter altogether and this varies between countries and is generally a highly contested and problematic issue. In the UK at this time the age of criminal responsibility is ten years, and children between ten and seventeen years can be arrested and tried in court. They are treated differently from adults (those eighteen years and above) and are tried, punished and remanded through the youth justice system. Certain projects and programmes are available to young people involved in crime or at risk of becoming involved such as a youth inclusion and support panel (YISP) or youth inclusion programme (YIP), and parents may be invited or required via a parenting order to attend a parenting programme by the local youth offending team (YOT). Parenting programmes are designed to help parents improve their skills in dealing with their child's behaviour and offer one-to-one advice and practical support.

See   https://www.gov.uk/age-of-criminal-responsibility for more information on the above in the UK.

Rights

The rules or laws for how we live in society are counter-balanced by rights and in 1948 the Universal Declaration of Human Rights was drafted by an international committee, representative of all parts of the world. For the first time the commitment to recognize and protect fundamental human rights across the globe was set down in statute and it was universally recognized that every human being needed certain rights to survive and to live with dignity and respect. Over four decades later, in 1989, the rights of children under eighteen years of age were ratified and specified under the United Nations Convention on the Rights of the Child (UNCRC). These rights include civil, cultural, economic, political and social rights as well as aspects of humanitarian law that just apply to children. The UNCRC forms the basis for everything that the United Nations Children's Fund (UNICEF) does to support children and to uphold children's rights all over the world.

Article 1 of the UNCRC states: 'If you are under eighteen years of age, you are a child, and you have rights.' It states that even though the rights of the child are very similar to those of adults, there is an additional requirement placed upon adults and governments to ensure that under eighteens can access their rights, as they are at a formative stage of life in which they are growing and learning and need additional protection.

The UNICEF website* describes the four guiding principles of the Convention, which are core requirements for any and all rights to be realized. The principles are:

- Non-discrimination: the 42 articles in the UNCRC relate to the rights of *every* child, no matter their religion, race or abilities; whatever they think or say; what their culture is; whether they are boys or girls or whether they are rich or poor

- The best interests of the child: any decision that is made, or any action that is taken, that may affect children must prioritize the best interests of the child, always

- Ensuring the child's survival and development: every child has the inherent right to life, and it is the responsibility of decision makers to ensure they are provided every opportunity to develop and reach their potential

- Participation: children are experts in their own lives and experiences, and should be consulted on decisions that affect them. Every child has the right to express his or her opinion, and can provide advice and valuable

---

* https://www.unicef.org.au/our-work/information-for-children

insight into how their rights can best be protected and fulfilled.

Although the majority of teenagers are unlikely to have actually researched and read about how their legally sanctioned human rights are important for daily life, I am struck by how often young people challenge the adults with whom they are involved for falling short of some or all of the above. However, I am also very much aware that the adults have to achieve a difficult balance of care and control and can easily get this wrong.

THINK ABOUT IT Try putting the last core right – participation – into practice right now and ask your young person what they know about the UNCRC. Choose a moment when they and you are relaxed and don't make it in any way like a teaching session. In the spirit of open-minded, genuine curiosity ask them if they have heard about it and if they have touched on it in their personal, social, health and economic education (PSHE) lessons at school. Make the point that you are interested to know if they've thought about it and talk about it in terms of their own lives. You could read the four core principles above and then ask them what it means for them personally in factual terms, emotional terms and also in relation to how they think things might be better for:

- Themselves right now
- Themselves in the future in their dealings with under eighteen year olds
- Their school
- Society as a whole.

Depending on the young person's interest and engagement you might find that this turns into a number of conversations, but suspend all expectations of how they will react – *stay open-minded*.

---

3. Parenting teenagers and what psychology can offer to parents

What is psychology?

The word psychology comes from two ancient Greek words *psyche*, meaning soul, spirit, breath, and *logia*, meaning study of, research. The earliest recorded use of the word psychology comes from the late 17th century in *The Physical Dictionary* by Steven Blankaart, which refers to anatomy and psychology, thereby distinguishing between the body and soul.

Nowadays, the many definitions of psychology available emphasize different aspects of the following:

- *The science of mental life of individuals and groups of all kinds including families*, with a focus upon mental processes such as thought, learning, memory, emotion, and on behaviour, including the social and societal factors affecting this. Scientific methods and methodologies are employed, that include measurement, assessment, observation, interview and testing.

- *A social science* that seeks to understand the wider social context in which problems can develop and in so doing seeks to address social issues.

- *An academic discipline* organized in relation to a particular theory or theories and system or systems of psychology generating psychological knowledge and understanding that is also informed by physiological and biological theory.

- *A professional practice* – the study of mind and behaviour in relation to a particular field of knowledge or activity, for example, clinical psychology, counselling psychology, educational psychology, forensic psychology or neuropsychology.

It's clear that psychology's remit and reach is huge and it is a testament to its rapid development and dissemination that society has in many ways absorbed the ideas and understandings generated by it.

As a professional psychologist I sometimes wince when I hear language generated from the study and practice of psychology used in a loose and inaccurate way, for example, when people describe themselves or others as 'phobic', 'dyslexic', 'psychotic', 'depressed', 'OCD' etc. However, the fact that such complex psychological conditions are used in such a matter-of-fact way, with such frequency, by all manner of individuals from different fields of human activity, be it advertising, media, commerce or politics, to name a few, suggests that the work of psychologists has made its mark on society's consciousness and therefore is affecting both the thinking and behaviour of people. This is not without its problems and often contributes to the view that many critics and sceptics hold:

Popular psychology is a mass of cant, of slush and of superstition worthy of the most flourishing days of the medicine man.

Philosopher and educationalist John Dewey
(1859–1952), from *The Public and Its Problems*

Hopefully, I can convince you in the pages to come that professional psychology offers something very much more positive and useful.

What kind of psychology does this book offer?

This book is written from a perspective that embraces all of the psychology-defining elements above, i.e. the science of mental life of individuals and groups of all kinds including families, a social science, an academic discipline and a professional practice.

Applied psychologists like myself often describe their work with children, young people, parents and individual adults, groups and organizations as 'research in practice'. This work involves drawing upon the theory and research in order to formulate ways of helping with complex processes of development, educational success, optimal performance, achievement and well-being. Writing about this work for a wide audience is a way of contributing to what one of the founders of humanist psychology had to say about psychology in general:

Only the understanding of human nature by every human being can be the proper goal for the science of human nature.

Alfred Adler, from
Understanding Human Nature (1927)

Parenting teenagers

In no order of things is adolescence the simple time of life.

Janet Erskine Stuart, Roman Catholic
nun and educator (1857–1914)

As I wrote earlier, the terms 'teen', 'teenager' and 'teenage' are all relatively modern terms first used in the middle of the 20th century. According to Skeat's *A Concise Etymological Dictionary of the English Language*, written originally in 1882, the etymological basis of the word 'teen' is English and means 'grief' or vexation. Certainly the commonly aired, stereotypical view of teenagers and the task of parenting them might be said to embody this meaning and the inherent potential for conflict and complexity. As a psychologist I am sceptical about this entirely negative viewpoint, often expressed in the media and the arts and also arising from much academic and clinical research focused very largely on the most problematic teenagers. It is important to remember that the large majority of teenagers, even the most difficult ones, make it through to adulthood and lead perfectly functional and satisfying lives and even go on to parent their own teenagers.

THINK ABOUT IT Think about all the teenagers that you have ever known who are now adults, including yourself. Rank these in terms of how 'difficult'/'problematic' they were, on a scale of one to ten, ten being the most difficult and one being the least. Now rank them in terms of the adult lives they are currently living, i.e. in terms of being generally functional and satisfying. What do you notice?

In my own professional and personal experience, many parents of teenagers can feel at a loss as to how to deal with the complex issues their young people experience and present to them. In addition, they can be experiencing feelings of disempowerment and insecurity as parents because they fear the loss of closeness and connection that parenting younger children entails, and also have less and less control. This may well arise from parents' lack of understanding about and knowledge of the social context that their children are dealing with, as they grew up in another, quite different world – one that did not feature the technology of today and all the implications that holds for the information young people can access: communication; social, albeit largely virtual, interaction opportunities; leisure time options and entertainment.

The quote from Janet Erskine Stuart on page 29 highlights the complexity of teenagers but complex doesn't have to mean problematic. One of my key ideas is that parents need to be engaged in continuous, everyday problem-solving and solution-finding, so now that I've touched upon the possible challenges, i.e. the problems, which of course I will return to, I want to move on to the opportunities and pleasures that are also possible and the big questions that thoughts about these prompt.

The pleasures and opportunities that can come from parenting teenagers

Here's my list:

- An increasing sense of the unique individual you have brought into the world and cared for over time, who is likely to express different, interesting and fresh views

- A relationship that has developed over time, involves a shared history and a great deal of authenticity and personal congruence on both sides

- The possibility of understanding yourself better, especially when you think about your younger self and the similarities and differences with your teenage child

- The possibility of understanding other people better in general

- The possibility of understanding the world better from a new angle

- Contact with the energy, passion and idealism of youth

- An opportunity to feel a sense of achievement and pride in your years of parenting work.

 This can be a one-off activity if you just do the first point or one that you do over time via a daily or even weekly journal. It can also be done with the other parent or any other adults involved:

1. Consider the teenager in question as a whole – their physical, emotional, social, spiritual, practical and academic skills and behaviour in general. Think of three things that you particularly like about them. Interestingly, this may well be things that you believe are true of yourself, or that you wish were true.

   ....

   ....

   ....

2. Depending upon the timescale that you are working to, make an entry in your journal every time you notice your teenager exhibiting one of the three positives you first listed.

3. After three weeks, start to record any positive changes you have noticed in: a) the teenager, b) yourself in relation to the teenager and c) other people in relation to the teenager and to yourself.

Positive psychology

Positive psychology is a broad term and approach, first used by American psychological theorist and researcher Martin Seligman, that can be defined and used in a number of different ways. However, according to Peterson (2008), who has researched the use of positive psychology with counselling American high school students, the most common and accepted definition is:

> *'Positive psychology is the scientific study of what makes life most worth living.'*

Positive psychology is characterized by:

- A scientific approach to the study of human thoughts, feelings and behaviour

- A focus upon the strengths and solutions rather than the weaknesses and problems

- Working towards a better and good life rather than repairing, fixing and mending bad lives

- A focus on positive experiences, e.g. joy, inspiration and love

- Positive attitudes, character dispositions and esteem, e.g. gratitude, resilience and compassion

- Positive organizations and institutions, i.e. ones which are founded upon and use positive principles such as focusing on achievement, strengths and virtues and finding ways of using them to the full.

The big questions

An important principle in positive psychology is that having once identified some strengths and positives about a situation or issue, as you have done in the above exercise, the next step is to analyse and better understand what makes these possible and in so doing find ways of increasing or amplifying positive characteristics or behaviours. We will be looking at ways of doing this further on in the book. I will also draw upon ideas from humanist psychology, which emphasizes the individual's unique perspectives, values, sense-making and personal resources in determining and working towards change, which will again prove important in supporting parents' relationships with their teenagers. I have found in my practice that this perspective and way of working does justice to the complexity of people's lives, is ethically principled, generally results in high levels of engagement from those being supported and produces some realistic and practical positive change. Another important humanist psychology idea for this book is that almost all human behaviour is driven by the need to achieve, to belong and to have some control, and below I list some of the big questions that I frequently hear from parents of teenagers that are directly related to these three areas of need. Chapters 4 and 5 will go into more detail about these ideas and theories.

Achievement

? How can you help teenagers to identify their strengths and gifts?

? How can you support teenagers in developing the attitudes and behaviours that are needed to develop these strengths and gifts?

? How do you help teenagers deal with sometimes not achieving or failing to meet their own and others' expectations?

Belonging

? How can you support teenagers in making relationship and social choices that are 'for their good'?

? How can you help teenagers build the personal confidence and self-love that are necessary for positive relationships with anyone else?

? How do you help teenagers learn from mistakes and difficulties in their social lives?

Control

? How much choice should teenagers have in terms of their relationships, lifestyles, health and behaviour in general?

? When is it appropriate to control a teenager's choices more or less?
? What should you do where a teenager appears to be 'out of control', i.e. taking back your control as a parent?

This book will offer ideas and suggestions for parenting teenagers that incorporate the following key themes that arise from humanist psychology and positive psychology, in particular:

- There are many positive aspects of parenting teenagers
- Your unique teenager has strengths, abilities and positive characteristics, which need to be remembered and used to care for and support them
- If you want to understand teenagers' behaviour bear in mind that nearly all of it, both desirable and undesirable, is driven by their need to achieve, belong and have some control.

Positive psychology
- A broad term and scientific approach, first used by Martin Seligman
- A focus upon the strengths, virtues and solutions in people's lives rather than the weaknesses and problems
- A focus upon and utilization of positive experiences, personal qualities and attitudes

- Working towards the positive in life rather than looking back at the problematic
- Identifying and amplifying the prerequisites of success and achievement and using this knowledge to the full.

Positive, individualized and practically useful ideas and suggestions

In the next chapter, Chapter 4, I am going to outline some of the particular psychological theories and approaches that inform my work, but for now I want to give a flavour of what readers can expect from this book, so here's the first case study.

William, aged thirteen years – a boy who learnt differently

When I meet a young person for the first time I make it a priority to ask about their strengths and positive qualities. I also listen to a range of people involved and hear about their experiences with the teenager, which almost always vary, sometimes in nature, sometimes by degree and sometimes both of these. For example, in this situation, I asked the question:

'Tell me about the times when William's difficulties with attention, behaviour and getting on with peers are not so evident.'

William's ICT, design and technology, and food technology teachers all reported a version of him that suggested a boy who could follow rules, listen and behave well and achieve good results. This was a completely different story to what I heard from teachers of the more academic subjects such as English, modern languages, history and maths. His science teacher also had good things to say about him whenever practical work was undertaken.

William himself talked with positivity about ICT, design and technology, food technology and science and so we talked about how he worked well with others in these classes, liked his teachers and found it easy to focus and behave well. Then we moved on to his *life out of school*. It is often the case that yet other versions of the young person are evident and sometimes one who is even harder to manage. This might be because the structures and boundaries aren't as clearly defined or agreed as at school, or it could be because someone else's needs are complicating the situation or again, it might just be that the young person feels secure enough to be their 'worst' and most challenging self. *Every case is different and the only way to find out is by asking questions.* There isn't room here for the detail of William's family and community life but suffice to say he was the youngest child and only boy, with sisters and a father who were all academic high-flyers. His mother was a successful graphic designer.

William told me that *he wanted to change how he got on with others.* The issues to do with attention and school rules weren't his priorities at that point. Another important detail was that his mum had been assessed as a child and found to have marked specific learning difficulties of a dyslexic nature. Along with the consultation I did some standardized testing of William's school achievement levels and cognitive capacities as well as other things. I found that in many, but not all, ways, he had the same profile of learning differences as his mother. It is definitely the case that every child, young person and adult has their own unique profile of learning style and capacity but it is also, in my experience, the case that family members can share similar profiles and the research supports this, for example, Snowling et al.'s study of children at family risk of dyslexia (2007).

When I told William about my findings he became upset and angry, saying there was nothing wrong with his brain and he wasn't 'thick like some of the other kids', as most of his teachers and his dad and sisters thought. I told him, far from lacking the ability to learn he actually had some clear strengths. I went into some detail about these and I also talked a bit about dyslexia, explaining that as more and more research was done it was showing that not only did between three and four people in every twenty experience dyslexia, but there was a lot of evidence to show that many of them were very bright and even had special gifts and abilities, hence the fact that some famous people are known for their creativity and original thinking styles and the special contributions they made to society.

So here's a summary of what William's case illustrates about the way psychology can help a teenager. It can:

- Look for strengths and positive aspects
- Listen to the difficulties from a range of sources relating to a variety of contexts and activities
- Note the different viewpoints
- Be curious about all of the above
- Find out what the young person wants most and highlight where and when they already have this
- Remember that the issues to do with self-worth, feelings and relationships, if addressed, make all difficulties more possible to address.

And by the way, William made huge progress after this educational psychology intervention, which identified his strengths and successes and raised his awareness of the positive aspects of his unique learning profile, as well as clarified and offered some practical suggestions for addressing his learning differences and related social and behavioural issues.

THINK ABOUT IT

Google famous gifted dyslexics – you will probably be surprised by the huge contribution to society made by individuals with learning differences.

4. Psychological theories and approaches

About theory

Psychologist, therapist and educationalist George Kelly, who created personal construct theory, said much about theory in general. His definition of theory was that of building together a quantity of facts in a way that made all the component facts possible to understand together and simultaneously, and then using this structure to predict in a reasonably precise, even scientific, way, what might happen in everyday life. Kelly originally studied mathematics and physics and his own theory-making undoubtedly draws upon and reflects this, thus illustrating one of the most important underlying ideas behind his own theory-making – that each individual can only make and use meaning from the understanding and experiences that they already possess. However, we all develop our understanding on a daily basis, whether or not we intend to do so, through the very process of living and the fact that no two days are ever exactly the same. Of course, some people, because of their particular situations, may have less variety in their day-to-day life than others, but if you look closely even the most routine-bound and limited physical circumstances are affected by variable aspects, for example, the weather, political and economic conditions, the individual's and others' mood states and actions. If you are the parent of a teenager or in any way involved with teenagers you will be aware of this more than most.

As a psychologist I have studied and continue to study different theories on a daily basis. I have also had the opportunity to talk with and try to understand the theories of many people, including the children, young people and adults with whom I have worked, and of other professionals and colleagues. Much as I appreciate, respect and use the theories generated by research and the academic field, I agree with Kelly that nearly all people create and use their own theories for living and these arise from their own life experiences as well as what they read and hear about. In our information-rich world of new technologies we have more and more to draw upon. For teenagers and the adults with whom they are involved there is a bewildering and huge amount of material available to consume.

Think about the last week: the contacts and conversations you have had with others; the viewing, reading and listening material with which you have been engaged. Are you able to list these accurately and in full? It is unlikely, given our multi-sensory and ever-changing world, but have a go, and then think about the following questions:

- What new thoughts/ideas/theories did your last week of life bring?

- Can you perhaps share one of these with your teenager?

- Can you perhaps ask them if they have had any new thoughts/ideas/theories recently?

The exercise above may not be possible at this time if your present relationship and/or communication with your teenager does not allow it, but it is still worth attempting as it communicates some important messages, showing that you want to learn, that you think learning is always important and possible and that you can learn from others including younger people:

> When I was a boy of fourteen, my father was so ignorant I could hardly stand to have the old man around. But when I got to be twenty-one, I was astonished at how much he had learned in seven years.
>
> Mark Twain (1835–1910)

Some of the theories that I use

> Complete systems and schemes of psychological explanation are the biggest stumbling-block in psychology.
> F.C. Bartlett in *A History of Psychology in Autobiography*, Vol. 3 (1936)

Although psychology is a relatively new field of study, research and knowledge, I want to highlight the fact that every theory is a work in progress, has developed from theories that precede it, and cannot claim to be complete and totally comprehensive for all aspects and types of human behaviour and the situations and contexts in which they arise. Psychologists as much as anyone else have to stay open-minded and attempt to be creative in their use of theory, and for each individual with whom they work they must use a research methodology, which is always underpinned by theory, or, more accurately, theories, and is organized by the particular questions that have given rise to them being involved. Some fictional and very exaggerated vignettes illustrating the sole use of each of the four major psychological theories follow. These 'grand theories', as they are known, include behaviourist, psychodynamic, humanist and cognitive theories.

Behaviourist theory
Behaviourist theory is based upon the principle that people, regardless of age, situation or individual characteristics, do more of a certain type of behaviour if they get rewarded for it, or less if they are punished.

Tom, a thirteen year old who won't help with household chores

Tom is the oldest son of parents Megan and Frank, both working full-time and raising their family of three boys. They are struggling to get

Tom to do some chores around the house such as taking out the rubbish, helping clear up after meals and general tidying up at the end of the day.

If I was using a purely behaviourist approach to change Tom's behaviour I would:

- Focus entirely on Tom's observable behaviour at this time, very much in the manner that experiments on animals are undertaken

- Measure and record what he is and isn't doing through observation, diary sheets and discussion with everyone involved

- Set up a system of rewards, e.g. extra pocket money or special activities for when Tom does help with the chores

- Set up a system of sanctions for when he does not help with the chores

- Identify the most successful measures of reward and sanctions as well as the ones that are not successful and modify the system of rewards and sanctions accordingly.

I would not:

- Take into account the adult models of helping round the house or the behaviour of his siblings

- Investigate what is happening in Tom's life outside home, i.e. at school and in his leisure time out and about

- Find out about and take into account Tom's or anyone else's feelings and relationships in the home

- See this aspect of Tom's behaviour as any different from an animal used in a laboratory-based study such as a rat, pigeon or dog.

 REMEMBER THIS!!! Pure behaviourist theory has developed from studies with animals in laboratories, which have been generalized to humans. The key idea is that people, regardless of age, situation or individual characteristics, do more of a certain type of behaviour if they get rewarded for it, or less if they are punished.

Psychodynamic theory
Psychodynamic theory and approaches entail the therapeutic exploration of early memories, feelings, fears and wishes over time and are dependent upon the ongoing relationship between client and therapist.

 CASE STUDY

Sara, a sixteen year old who steals
Sara is a bright girl who is doing well at school, has many friends and seems to be content and full of energy. Sara's mum, Camilla, gives her daughter, an only child, what she views as

46

reasonable pocket money but has found out that Sara is regularly helping herself to money from her own purse. She also discovered a couple of garments with security tags still attached under Sara's mattress and so suspects her of shoplifting as well.

If I was using a purely psychodynamic approach in this scenario I would:

- Talk with Camilla about her feelings to do with her pregnancy with Sara and Sara's development, Camilla's own childhood and family situation

- Talk with Camilla about her relationships with others involved with Sara as well as with Sara

- Talk with Sara about her feelings and relationships with her mum, other relatives, friends and anyone else with whom she is involved

- Possibly use some free association techniques using art, discussion and make-believe scenarios

- Refer on to an appropriate professional who could offer in-depth therapy over time.

I would not:

- Attempt any other investigation of the views of others about Sara's behaviour, i.e. school staff or other family members

- Work with anyone other than Sara and Camilla

- Attempt to measure frequency and degree of stealing behaviour
- Undertake any individualized standardized assessment of Sara's cognitive capacities or academic achievement
- Observe or visit any contexts other than Sara's home
- Focus on achieving targeted outcomes that can be specified, measured and timed.

Interventions based on a purely psychodynamic theoretical approach entail the commitment of much time, exploration of early memories, feelings, fears and wishes and are dependent upon the ongoing relationship between client and therapist.

Humanist theory
In humanist theory, the individual's unique perspectives, values and sense-making are central to determining and working towards change and their own resources are key.

Michelle, a fifteen year old who is very shy

Michelle is the middle child of Rona and Leslie's three adopted children. She joined the family after her biological parents were killed in a car crash. As a young child she was outgoing, sociable and popular. Since starting secondary school she has become increasingly isolated and withdrawn and spends most of her time playing computer games and reading.

If I was using a purely humanist approach to work through this situation I would:

- Work from the premise that all individuals strive to achieve, belong and have some control over their lives

- Understand that many factors and complexities, both within and external to Michelle, affected her perceptions, attributions and behaviours

- View and affirm Michelle's own meaning-making about herself and the world as more important than objective, observable behaviour

- Devise all discussions and activities with Michelle in order to ensure that her unique meaning-making was clear and this would be used as the starting point for all interventions

- Recognize that my own perspective (e.g. on how sociable a young person should be) needs to be influenced by Michelle's beliefs, experiences and the challenges and opportunities of her current situation

- Try not to impose my own values and norms for adolescent behaviour as a measure of successful intervention

- Agree with Michelle what changes were a priority.

I would not:

- Classify Michelle in any clinical or cognitive sense, i.e. with a mental health disorder or learning disability
- Give precedence to the views of others involved with Michelle over her own sense-making
- Give precedence to the objectivity, rigour and measurement of scientific method
- Set specific outcome targets.

In humanist theory, the individual's unique perspectives, values and sense-making are central to determining and working towards change and their own resources are key.

Cognitive theory

Cognitive theory is concerned with perception, thinking, learning and problem-solving and behavioural change is based upon material gained about the characteristics of individuals concerned from this perspective.

Leon, a fourteen year old who never completes his written work at school

Leon is a very sporty and active boy who is a star of his football teams both within and outside of school. He is the younger son of David and Maria, both of whom work as healthcare assistants. Leon's

50

teachers throughout his schooling have complained that he writes as little as possible and often does not finish his work.

If I was using a purely cognitive approach when working with Leon I would:

- View Leon's difficulties in terms of performance and information-processing and therefore to a large degree as a result of the choices available to him

- Explore the arrangements for his learning, i.e. methods of teaching, physical learning conditions, rules for learning in operation and quality of information made available to him

- Use standardized cognitive individual assessment methods

- Use structured observation of Leon within his learning contexts, for example in classrooms

- Use my findings to articulate the schemas (rules) by which Leon learns best and, conversely, those which hamper or reduce his learning

- Devise an individualized learning programme with specific, measurable, achievable, relevant and timed (SMART) targets for implementation at school.

I would not:

- Explore Leon's feelings and relationships or the views about these with parents and/or school staff

- Explore the attitudes to learning and academic achievement, including the values attributed to these by Leon and significant others in his life apart from school staff

- Conduct any assessment that is not standardized, i.e. based upon statistical probability as deemed by measures taken from a sample of same-age young people

- Explore the context for Leon's learning in any way other than as manifest in his individual performance.

REMEMBER THIS!!! Cognitive theory is concerned with perception, thinking, learning and problem-solving. It views human behaviour like a complex computer or machine and research is designed to break the code and system by which the computer works and then make the necessary changes for optimal achievement.

---

*

As I have written these imaginary vignettes it has been difficult to resist repeating my disclaimer that applied psychologists select and draw upon many theoretical approaches in their real-world practice. My separation of each of the four major theories is an artificial and very crude exercise as in reality the ideas contributing to a theory originate and develop from all or some of the theories of behaviourist, psychodynamic, humanist or cognitive psychology. In addition, some theories that are used in applied psychology practice do not fit neatly into these four main categories, so in the next chapter when I write about areas of particular challenge for the parents of adolescents and make some suggestions that may help, I explain some other theories.

---

1. Psychology is a science, an academic discipline and a kind of professional practice

2. Psychology aims, through the application of scientific methods and theory, to describe, understand and improve the behaviour, experience, development, learning and well-being of individuals and groups of all kinds

3. Psychological research builds upon existing research and theory in order to create even better theories and research and to generalize about particular aspects of human existence

4. Four main theoretical frameworks have developed: behaviourist, psychodynamic, humanist and cognitive.

---

5. Theories that help us understand the teenage journey

The teenage years are often described as a journey and this metaphor works on so many levels because, like a journey, teenagers:

- Must make the transition from one place – childhood – to another – adulthood
- Can take an infinite variety of routes
- Can travel by different means
- Will incur costs and gains
- Will encounter setbacks and also periods of calm
- May take shortcuts
- Will be tested
- Will learn and develop
- Usually have companions
- Sometimes have mentors/guides
- Generally need an adult driver/pilot/captain who may or may not be following a map or route guide.

Think about your teenager's journey and what it has meant to you in terms of the points above.

I also like this way of thinking about teenagers conveys the movement, the physicality and the k of being alive that epitomize the teenage years, ve as in this poem:

> To move, to breathe, to fly, to float,
> To gain all while you give,
> To roam the roads of lands remote:
> To travel is to live
>
> Hans Christian Andersen, writer, best
> known for his fairy tales, from *The Fairy Tale
> of My Life, An Autobiography*, 1847

Theoretical models

Various theoretical models emphasizing different aspects and ways of thinking about the journey of *adolescent development* have been created, which arise from the four grand theories of psychology referred to in the previous chapter: behaviourist, psychodynamic, humanist and cognitive. Here's a summary of seven key theories proposed by Nicolson and Ayres (2004) in their book about adolescent problems (see references):

1. **Erik Erikson**'s work places *identity* as central to the developmental challenges of adolescence, which in turn contributes to a person's process of life-long growth. He viewed the interaction of what the individual adolescent brings, i.e. biological and psychological make-up

with cultural and social experiences and choices, as underpinning the individual's identity. He proposed eight stages of psycho-social development throughout life and the fifth of these, which takes place in adolescence, is that of *identity versus role confusion*. His work is most closely allied to psychodynamic theory.

2. **Lawrence Kohlberg** created a model of adolescent development that hinges upon the development of *moral reasoning intrinsic to personal identity*. He built upon cognitive theory and suggested a six-stage hierarchy of moral development. This starts with the pre-moral stage of the very young child, aged four to ten years, whose moral reasoning is driven by expectations of personal reward or fear of punishment, through an intermediate conventional moral stage, ten years and onwards, of moral judgement or choice-making defined by authorities who dictate and regulate what is right and wrong, and then as adulthood begins an autonomous stage, where the individual exercises their own personal choice about what is right and wrong that is no longer based upon personal interests, approval of others or conforming with external rules and values. Most adolescents journey through the second stage and ideally into the third stage as they mature and the remaining three stages, post-conventional, human rights and morality of ethical principles, are generally engaged with to different degrees by adults.

3. **Jane Loevinger**'s ideas use the concept of *ego*, a psychodynamic term, and the development of meaning and coherence in relation to this. Her stages of development span pre-social, symbiotic, impulsive, self-protective, conformist, self-awareness, conscientious, individualistic, autonomous and integrated. These stages are not necessarily discrete and the journey to ego maturity not necessarily in this order. Loevinger used statistically based methods and materials to measure individual development and on the basis of her assessments claimed that adolescents rarely operated at a level of autonomy or integrated ego development, i.e. where they exercise their own considered moral judgement and behaved and thought in a mature, balanced and measured way.

4. **Albert Bandura** is known for his *social-cognitive approach*, which, in a nutshell, views the adolescent and also the adult in active and meaning-making interactions with their environment. This theory links with psychodynamic, behaviourist and cognitive theories. Bandura's premise is that the individual's biological and psychological make-up, the environment and the behaviour of the individual all act upon and influence each other. There is no clear distinction between adolescent and adult and therefore no developmental staged model of maturation is offered, but instead the emphasis is placed upon the social and physical environments,

including phenomena such as behavioural choices and styles influenced by models of adult behaviour, the influence of media and society at large.

5. **Urie Bronfenbrenner**'s ideas about adolescent development are based upon an *ecological* perspective and have strong links with the social-cognitive model as described above, because he saw all behaviour as arising from and relating to the individual in interaction with their environment. He called this a process–person–context model and categorized the context as consisting of four interrelated and interacting parts: the microsystem, i.e. face-to-face social interactions such as with family, friends, neighbours and school; the mesosystem, the interactions between groups categorized by the microsystems such as age, for example, adolescents and parents; the ecosystem, which is the local community or local authority to which the adolescent belongs, i.e. the school, the locality in which they live and the workplace; and finally, the macrosystem, which is the entire system in which the adolescent exists and encompasses social mores and cultural values and defines and legislates adolescent status and rights. Bronfenbrenner saw problems arising where communication is poor or non-existent between microsystems, there is no agreed basis of values and where some aspects of the adolescents' microsystem, i.e. other teenagers, legitimize and approve of behaviour that is

illegal or at odds with the values, rules and laws of other microsystems, e.g. school, local community or parents.

6. **Peter Blos** used a psychodynamic view of adolescent personality development and related the challenges of adolescence to the *Oedipal complex*, a term that comes from the Greek legend in which a son kills his father and marries his mother. There is a female equivalent, the Electra complex; the story tells of another mythological character who helped slay her own mother. From this basis Blos believed that the main challenges of adolescence are to separate from the identification with parents, to cope with and resolve, psychologically, past traumas, to have a sense of continuing identity or ego over time and to develop a sexual identity.

7. **Robert Kegan**'s model of adolescent development focuses on *adolescent identity formation*, and again draws upon psychodynamic theory, particularly the concept of subject–object relations, i.e. the young person as knower or thinker and the object of their thoughts and/or basis of knowing. For Kegan, the young person's meaning-making and sense of self are key and the focus of this widens as the child matures – from within their own unconscious self to themselves in the wider world and society.

THINK ABOUT IT

1. I've linked the above seven models of adolescent development to the four grand theories: behaviourist, psycho-dynamic, humanist and cognitive.

2. Of the four grand theories psychodynamic features the most, which is hardly surprising as identity/ego/person-ality development is very much central to psychody-namic theory and to teenagers.

3. Most of the models focus on the inner processes and development of individual teenagers but Bronfenbrenner's and Bandura's models place an emphasis upon the social context and situation.

Which models of adolescent development make sense to you when you think back to your own teenage years?

Section 2:
The major issues

6. Achievement

We return now to the central premise of this book, mentioned briefly within Chapter 3, which is that nearly all aspects of an adolescent's behaviour are linked to their wish to achieve, belong and to have some control/choice. Although all three are interlinked, we will look first at achievement, and this will be illustrated with two case studies. Further case studies to illustrate specific problems relating to achievement will follow in the next section.

What does the teenager need to achieve?

Generally speaking, the average teenager needs and wants to achieve their own unique identity; physical and cognitive growth; well-being and capacity; a range of cognitive, social and emotional skills and a level of performance in relation to these that allows them to feel successful and that fulfils their potential as much as possible. On top of this, towards the end of adolescence, teenagers want to achieve some economic and practical independence and to be increasingly confident as they exercise this. Obviously, parents of teenagers also want to have a sense of achievement and their own agendas may include aspects of their work, past, current and future; aspects of an economic nature; material possessions such as cars and property; holidays; hobbies and sports and, of course, their own parenting. This can sometimes result in conflicting priorities within the family.

Susan, eighteen years old – a young woman who dreams of being a champion swimmer

Susan came from a sporting family; her mother had been a county youth tennis champion and met her father at university where they both studied sports science.

Both parents continued to play tennis and encouraged their two daughters to do the same from an early age, but at eight years of age Susan had discovered she was an excellent swimmer. Susan's younger sister Helen had stuck to the tennis and showed every sign of being at least as good as her mother. Family life tended to be organized around the tennis and during the summer one or both parents would accompany Helen to tournaments and practice sessions all over the country. This included Susan until she was about twelve, when her own interests took over. Susan was encouraged to keep up her tennis practice as her parents reasoned that it would help with her swimming, they understood what was required of an aspiring tennis champion and anyway it was a lot easier to fit into their busy schedule. This also ceased when she was about twelve. The pool at which Susan was a member was much further away than the tennis club and from her early teens Susan found her own way there via two buses and walking. When she was involved in galas and competitions she was frequently one of the few young people who did not have family members present.

At eighteen, Susan was babysitting for several families and had a job in the local shopping centre, the earnings used largely to fund her sport as the family resources were almost entirely used on her younger sister's tennis. Her parents had very much opposed her choice to not stay on at school and do A levels as she had been a very able student, but grudgingly acceded to their daughter's wishes. Susan was staying at various swimming friends' houses more nights a week than at home and her health began to suffer with frequent colds and stomach upsets. This in turn resulted in her swimming excellence decreasing and she was dropped from the club's squad. One of the swimming friends' fathers – a GP – and the swimming club coach became so concerned that they both called Susan's mother, who was already feeling guilty, blamed and took offence, blaming Susan for being disloyal and a disappointment to her own family. Susan's father was less critical and in many ways very sympathetic as his teenage years were rather similar to his daughter's as he had been ambitious to become a top golfer but his parents had made him compromise by persuading him to go to university.

So what is going on here and what is there to work with?

There's a huge amount going on in this simplified scenario. Perhaps it sounds quite intractable but actually, viewing it from a positive psychology perspective, there are many possibilities for helping to improve the situation. Whichever model of adolescent development you base your understanding upon, certain strong themes leap out:

- Sporting achievement is intrinsic to the whole family's self-worth and is highly valued

- Susan's chosen field of excellence, swimming, represents new ground to her family and one in which she alone has achieved skills and experience

- Susan has demonstrated discipline, hard work and resourcefulness in her passion for swimming and achieved some success

- In her quest for excellence Susan has compromised her physical health and well-being

- Susan has impressed people in her swimming circle and accessed social and emotional support that has not been available at home

- Susan's parents, particularly her father, are concerned and do want to help her.

- At the end of the chapter I will give my perspective but what do you think can be done to help this situation?

- Which models of adolescent development are useful for understanding this situation?

- What suggestions would you make?

Franco, thirteen years old – a boy who daydreams during lessons and does not get his work done

Franco is the third child of his parents, who have their own office-supplies business in which his two siblings, who are in their twenties, are employed. Both his older sister and brother are married with young families of their own. Franco did very well at primary school, was good at English and maths and was seen as a good all-rounder. He lives in an area of selective secondary schools and passed the 11+ examination and achieved a place at a highly academic school. Franco's parents both left school at fifteen and achieved their business success despite having no formal academic qualifications. However, both of Franco's siblings went to university and got good degrees, which have been very usefully employed in the family business – the brother is the company accountant and the sister manages human resources.

Franco's life is packed with activity that is carefully managed by his mother to synchronize with her work commitments. He plays football twice a week, goes to computer club, has piano lessons and is also a great chess player. On the days where he isn't at a club he attends an after-school homework club. Most weekday evenings the whole family, mum and dad, siblings and their families, eat together. Franco is a sociable, healthy and active boy who sleeps and eats well.

He is now in his second year of secondary school and every termly report since he started states that he is underachieving, daydreaming in lessons and not completing assignments. When asked what he is daydreaming about, his answer is 'nothing', 'don't know' or 'bored'. The school's educational psychologist (EP) was asked to work with Franco in order to advise staff and parents on how to improve the situation. She did some discussion-based and drawing activities in order to understand how Franco saw himself and his situation. Interestingly, his drawings featured two scenarios on the same sheet of paper, separated by a thick black felt-tip line of a classroom with other children at their desks and of him at home at the dinner table surrounded by family.

When the psychologist asked him to tell her about himself he talked about his activities, his family, his parents' business and his friends. He did not mention school at all and when asked about this had little to say about what he wanted from school or about future aspirations. Franco's parents attended a meeting, rather reluctantly, with his form tutor and head of year, after being asked by the school to do so on several occasions. They could see no issue with how their son was behaving and felt that the problem lay with the school.

So what is going on here and what is there to work with?

Again, this is a simplified scenario but there are many positives to report:

- Franco is a bright boy with no obvious learning difficulty
- Although he is experiencing attention difficulties and is not applying himself to formal schoolwork, he is able to engage and apply himself successfully to a wide range of activities outside of school
- He is sociable, healthy and active
- His school attendance and punctuality are fine
- Franco devotes his energies to other activities outside of school
- Franco's parents consider their son is fine and attribute the problem to how the school is managing his learning.

- What do you think can be done to help this situation?
- Which models of adolescent development and grand theories are useful for understanding Franco's situation?
- What suggestions would you make?

My perspectives on Susan's and Franco's situations

All seven of the models of adolescent development are useful and relevant for understanding these young people's situations. I have italicized key points from different theories within the case studies:

In *Susan*'s case it is clear that she is intent on securing her *identity and personal choices for development* (Erikson and Kegan) as an excellent swimmer. However, a conflict between her values associated with this and her family's (Bronfenbrenner) has given rise to an unequal distribution of her parents' time, money and energy between her and her sister, who is adhering to what the parents see as most valuable and therefore affirmative of their success as parents. Perhaps the parents' beliefs about swimming need to be reframed (redefined) as another equally valuable form of sporting achievement and in this way encourage them to become more involved and more knowledgeable about this sport. As I wrote, she has demonstrated discipline, hard work, sociability and resourcefulness in her passion for swimming and achieved some success, and she has also developed a degree of *autonomy* in her *moral reasoning* (Kohlberg) and *ego maturity* (Loevinger) in her ambitious quest for excellence. Bandura's ideas about the interlinked *social-cognitive* aspects of Susan's active and meaningful interaction with her social and physical environment as a would-be sporting champion does, at core, reflect the models of adult behaviour her parents have provided but again, there may be a lack of awareness about this on both Susan's and her parents' parts.

Finally, drawing upon the model created by Blos, if the family dynamics are considered, it could be possible, at some level, that Susan, in her efforts to separate from her mother and to reduce the identification with her, has chosen to go outside the tennis world to achieve sporting success, and again, work to view her developmental choices this way could be very beneficial. In terms of the sort of professional support to help Susan and her family, the most effective help might be in-depth therapy with the whole family over time so that they are helped to consider that Susan's ambitions and motivations might be viewed and actually encouraged as evidence of her growing up and developing her own unique identity. This in turn might be seen as evidence of successful parenting and in this way could restore the unity of the family as a whole.

In the case of *Franco*, his main difficulty appears to be about his engagement with schoolwork. He is a sociable, healthy and active boy and in all other aspects of his life there are no issues to do with his behaviour, attitudes, school attendance, punctuality or attention and his performance at primary school and out of school at this time is not raising any concerns, so what might be the problem? This is where it is helpful to widen the lens and take into account the fact that his parents blame the school for not interesting and engaging their son and that they have been reluctant to get involved. This is very much an example of what Bronfenbrenner's model of adolescent development emphasizes. In Franco's case *the microsystems* of his school, namely the teachers, and his family have not been working together or communicating effectively. Franco has chosen, not necessarily consciously, to ally with his parents' attitudes. The psychologist's intervention to increase Franco's engagement at school involved working with his parents, bringing teachers and parents together and highlighting the fact that everyone involved with Franco appreciated his talents and capacities and wanted him to fulfil his good potential. A breakthrough was achieved when Franco spoke of how he wanted to join the family business and some discussion took place about what his university-educated siblings were able to contribute and how he might add to this. He volunteered that he would like to study ICT and maybe help in that way, which delighted his parents. Kegan's model that centres around the young person's *meaning-making* and *sense of self* are key and the widening focus as s/he matures is very useful here.

Think about your own teenager/s and their priorities in terms of achievement and then think about yours. How much, if any, overlap is there? If possible have a relaxed conversation about this and ask in a very open-ended way if there is anything you can do to help or support them. Be prepared for the possibility that they don't have much to say initially and if so leave it and return at a later date. You can rest assured that a subject of this nature will register with them but they may need time; days, weeks or even months, before they have thought it through enough to have much to say.

---

7. Belonging

The second of the core motivations or needs, according to humanist theory, is belonging. To be human is to live in a social context, with and/or alongside other people. The social nature of humans is a defining characteristic and links with the development of language, the social drive, social behaviour and societal structures in general. Most children and adolescents gradually build layer upon layer of understanding, proficiency and skills in all of these areas by the time they are adults but some experience particular difficulties or even specific disorders, and I shall return to some of these in the next section along with issues such as sexuality, body image and bullying, actual and virtual. For now we will turn to two case studies that illustrate some general points around the need for belonging.

CASE STUDY

Millie, thirteen years old, a girl who finds it hard to make friends and tends to be shy

Millie had a difficult start in life, in that she was born a month early and required special baby care for several weeks before being able to leave hospital and go home with her mum and dad. She was their first child and neither parent had any extended family around as they were from America and had only been in the UK a matter

73

of weeks before Millie was conceived. Millie made good progress and met all of her developmental milestones and was a healthy and happy child. Understandably, her parents were very protective and decided not to send Millie to pre-school and her opportunities for socializing with other children were very limited. In addition, Millie had an August birthday, late in the school year, and so when she started formal education at four years and one month, not only was she physically very small but her language was not as developed as that of most of her classmates. She was distressed at being left by her mum or dad at school to begin with and had a very gradual and part-time programme for the first term, then successfully attended full-time. Thanks to very supportive and understanding teachers throughout her primary school and the fact that both her parents had flexible working-from-home arrangements she settled happily in time, her language development caught up with peers, she coped with the curriculum, gradually made a few school friends and showed a flair for art.

The transition to secondary school was not as straightforward but again, the commitment of teachers, the fact that one of her good friends was placed in the same tutor group and, in my view, the trust and faith of the parents in the school helped her through some difficult first months. At thirteen years and in her third year of secondary education, Millie was doing reasonably well with her schoolwork and again, she had made a few very strong friendships. However, it was the school's policy from Year 9 to set pupils in subjects and tutor groups according to their assessed ability and as all three of Millie's friends were academically extremely able, they were placed in top sets whereas she went into middle sets. This is when her tendency to be withdrawn, very quiet and shy and her difficulties with making new friends really became more pronounced and both teachers and parents became especially concerned. Millie's parents blamed themselves for being rather work-orientated and insular with few friends outside work. The school's home–school liaison officer visited Millie's parents and sought advice from the linked EP who provided some staff development sessions that gave the staff some ideas regarding how to help Millie. The EP also had a telephone consultation with Millie's parents.

So what is going on here and what is there to work with?

This is a simplified scenario but there are many positives to report:

- Millie's difficult start in life has resulted in her parents being very protective of her and she and her mother and father have developed an exceptionally close relationship

- On starting formal education at just over four years of age her language development was a little delayed and she found separation from her parents distressing, but in time with helpful school and parenting measures she settled happily at school and her development and learning progressed along age-appropriate lines

- The transition to secondary school was challenging for Millie but again, school measures, including being in a tutor group with one of her friends from primary school, helped and she settled, attended well and continued to progress

- When Millie started her third year of secondary education, in line with the school's policy, she was placed in different sets to and had less contact with her established friends so that she became withdrawn, very quiet and shy, but teachers and parents responded together quickly and devised effective ways of helping her.

- At the end of the chapter I will give my perspective but what ideas do you have for helping Millie?

- Which models of adolescent development are useful for understanding Millie's situation?

- What suggestions would you make to school, to the parents and to Millie?

CASE STUDY

Brandon, a fifteen year old who spends a lot of his time out of school playing computer games and watching internet material

Brandon is the middle child of three children who live with their parents in a large house some distance from his school. His older sister is at university and his younger sister is still at the primary school which Brandon previously attended and which is a couple of minutes away from his home. He now has a complicated hour-long journey involving two bus rides and a walk to his all-boys' secondary school. He amuses himself during the long bus journeys by listening through headphones to music and radio shows and chatting with friends from school. In school he is making steady progress, has a group of boys with whom he spends breaks and lunchtimes and his strongest subjects are science and maths. He has not joined any of the school's after-school activities and clubs and is not particularly interested in sports. Brandon's father works away during the week as a highly paid IT consultant and his mother has her own dressmaking business. At home Brandon is an organized and helpful boy who during the week seems to have taken on a lot of the household chores that his father would ordinarily do, for example, he helps his younger sister with her homework as well as doing his own. He earns his pocket money by happily emptying the dishwasher, doing his own washing, walking the dog, taking the rubbish out and cutting the grass, without even being asked.

Both parents have encouraged Brandon to bring friends home from school and to arrange social activities with school friends but he is uninterested in doing so and they are worried about the extent of his social isolation. Brandon's mother has met with his form tutor and head of year on a number of occasions and expressed her concerns but thinks that because her son's academic progress and behaviour is good she is viewed as being unnecessarily worried. In addition, school staff have observed Brandon with his peers and it is clear that although he is one of the quieter boys, he is not isolated or friendless. The school's EP holds a school-based workshop for parents every autumn to talk about general adolescent learning and development issues and Brandon's mother attended one of these but contributed very little to the discussion, which on this occasion was mainly about young people and drugs and alcohol. After the session she spoke with the EP and became very upset.

So what is going on here and what is there to work with?

The basic and largely positive situation is:

- Brandon is the middle child of three children who live with their parents in a large house some distance from his school and at home is happy and helpful

- He has a long journey to school during which he happily occupies himself

- In school he is making steady progress, has a group of boys with whom he spends breaks and lunchtimes and his strongest subjects are science and maths

- He has not joined any of the school's after-school activities and clubs and is not particularly interested in sports, preferring to get home as soon as he can

- Both parents have encouraged Brandon to bring friends home from school or to arrange social activities with them, but he is content with seeing his friends at school and spending time at home occupying himself and being with his family

- The school is pleased with Brandon's work and behaviour.

- Do you think Brandon needs help, and if so how?
- Which models of adolescent development are useful for understanding Brandon's situation?
- What suggestions would you make to the school, to the parents and to Brandon?

My perspectives on Millie's and Brandon's situations

Again I make links with the seven models of adolescent development outlined at the end of Section 1 in trying to understand these young people's situations and I have italicized key points from different theories within the case studies:

Millie is a child with *dependency and separation issues* (psychodynamic theory), which appear to heighten at times of change and transition, hence her difficulties when she started school, transferred to secondary education and then again in Year 9 when her class arrangements were adjusted in order to accommodate the GCSE syllabus. She clearly benefits from stability and continuity, as is the case for all children and young people, and it would appear from her history that if she can be helped to regain a sense of these she can become happy and settled and continue to learn and develop.

Erikson's model of psycho-social development is helpful here and states that the usual stage a thirteen year old would be grappling with would be that of identity versus role confusion, but Millie seems to be at an earlier stage in the sense that she has issues about *trust and mistrust*. She experiences anxiety and views the world as a fearful place when those with whom she has strong connections – her parents, her primary school teachers and her particular friends – are not available. Loevinger's psychodynamic ideas about ego development would suggest that Millie is operating in a somewhat symbiotic rather than self-aware and individualistic manner, i.e. she looks to others for a sense of self and security and her personal resources for widening her social support are limited. Millie's parents were actively encouraged to become more involved with the school through the parent–teacher association, and by doing this not only did they provide *positive adult models* of social behaviour for Millie, but widened the family's social circle and Millie became involved with other adults and their children at the many PTA holiday and weekend events.

Bronfenbrenner's *process–person–context model* – the idea that all behaviour arises from the individual in inter-action with their environment – leads me to think that Millie's situation cannot be explained by difficulties in communi-cation between home and school, the local or wider com-munity, but possibly by difficulties within the microsystem of her peer group. The EP thought that Millie had always taken a rather passive and dependent social position with peers and there might be some potential for changing this by asking her to become involved in mentoring younger students as they started at the secondary school.

Kegan's model of *adolescent identity formation* places the young person's meaning-making and sense of self as central, and suggests that ideally their focus will widen outwards to others and the world in general. Therefore the importance of Millie being helped to clarify and work towards her personal aspirations and future plans is another potential avenue for enabling her development and well-being. The EP suggested that teachers and Millie's parents encourage Millie to join some after-school activities such as the art club and also some projects linking with the local community, e.g. visiting a care home for the elderly.

Brandon seems happy and is doing well in all respects apart from his social development with peers. He is comfortably bonded to his family and has a clear and central role in the day-to-day life of the home. The fact that he sees no problem in not having a social life out of school is unusual and nearly every text written on adolescence highlights the tendency of most young people to want to spend increasing amounts of time with peers. When Brandon's mother disclosed her worries to the school's EP she spoke, with the mother's permission, with school staff, who confirmed that they had no particular concerns. The EP then arranged to meet with Brandon and was frank about her reason for doing so. Brandon was surprised but not hostile to talking about why he didn't socialize out of school. He explained that he was concerned about his mother being on her own all week and that he had decided she was his priority at this time. He also said that he was saving his pocket money up so that as soon as he was seventeen he could learn to drive and buy a car.

If we consider Brandon's sense of *identity* (Erikson, Kegan) he seems to have established a positive and robust one that serves him well in terms of his own *meaning-making*, priorities, lifestyle and chosen behaviour (Bandura). However, it is not in line with the expectations of the adults in his life and they are the ones who see this as a problem. After all, adolescents are supposed to be prioritizing relationships with peers at this time of life, and a boy who doesn't do this is seen as going short of the appropriate opportunities for social and emotional development. The EP put this perspective to Brandon and he was genuinely surprised. He explained that when he spent time on his computer and phone it was very often in the company of his friends from school – they communicated every day, shared material and engaged in interactive games for hours at a time.

Brandon seems to have developed a mature style of *moral judgement* (Kohlberg) in that he does not mind appearing to be making choices that are different to many of his peers, and has deliberately elected to take on the role of his absent father during the week. His *ego development* (Loevinger) also seems to be quite mature in that he is exhibiting quite a lot of self-awareness, conscientiousness, autonomy and independence.

In many ways Brandon's choices seemed perfectly reasonable but nevertheless, the fact that his mother and school staff held concerns was in itself a problem and therefore the EP decided that a useful approach might be to draw upon Bronfenbrenner's ideas and to facilitate better communication between the different microsystems at play. She arranged for a home–school review meeting to be held and actively encouraged Brandon's father to attend along with his mother and, if everyone was agreeable, Brandon also. In the event, Brandon decided he didn't want to be present but was happy for the meeting to take place and then talk with his parents about what had been discussed. As a result of the meeting a few actions were agreed:

1. Brandon arranged to stay one night a week with a friend who lived close to the school and the friend frequently came to stay at Brandon's house at weekends. Over time the arrangement was extended so that different friends became involved.

2. Brandon's father decided to match Brandon's savings towards his car and also told him that his seventeenth birthday present would be a course of driving lessons. This meant that Brandon had more spending power for when he was with friends.

3. The school decided to extend their parent support sessions and to run a course specifically on adolescent development run by their EP along with the home–school liaison officer.

THINK ABOUT IT

These case studies serve as a reminder of the importance of friendships and may remind you of friends from your own adolescence. Take a look at the acronym below and consider your own experiences past and present in terms of these points and how you perceived your own parents' thoughts on them:

All people, including adolescents, are socially motivated

Don't try to choose your children's friends, but instead be available to guide and discuss issues that come up within the friendships

Only children can become very used to adult company and will benefit from encouragement to socialize with other children

Listening skills are a key aspect of ...

Effective communication

Self-confidence is important

Congruence – truly being yourself – is equally, if not more, important

Enthusiasm and being happy are key personal qualities to be encouraged

Noticing and being concerned about others are also desirable and attractive qualities

Time – as children develop they usually spend increasing amounts of time with peers. When they don't there is usually a good reason that is worth exploring

Friendships serve a number of important functions:

Rescue from being bored and stimulation

Intimacy and affection

Ego support

Not being alone (unless this is wanted!) – companionship

Doing practical and physical activities together

Social comparison.

8. Control and choice

The third humanist core motivation is control and choice, and many of the problematic aspects of parenting teenagers are commonly associated with the struggles surrounding this need. On top of this, because of their stage of development and relatively little life experience, teenagers can often *feel* out of control:

> *Certainly old age has a great sense of calm and freedom: when the passions relax their hold, then, as Sophocles says, you have escaped from the control not of one master, but of many.*
>
> Plato (427–347 BC), *The Republic*

This quotation highlights the emotional highs and lows of being younger and there are scientific reasons backing this up. Although this book cannot cover the neurological and biological details of the adolescent stage of development, it is important to acknowledge that adolescent brain development means that not only is the young person striving to gain independence and to engage in new experiences, their capacity to control emotions is not fully developed. This capacity, for the vast majority, will come in time but the different ways people manage feelings are many and highly individual.

Because of the inherently social nature of being human, we tend to live and operate in groups, communities and organizations and this means that a multitude of different needs and wishes have to be accommodated. The law and situation-specific and activity-specific rules and regulations are formally outlined but there are many unspoken and unwritten rules for social behaviour that have to be learnt and assumed through experience and it is every individual's task to navigate and stay within these. For parents of teenagers, whose job it is to help and support their young people to grow into functional, productive, healthy and hopefully happy individuals, there can be many challenges. In this chapter I will again present two case studies that highlight some general and common issues relating to teenagers and control/choice. More specific issues that are closely linked to control/choice come in the next section of the book.

Karl, a fourteen year old who will not help at home

Karl has one sister, Jane, who is a year younger. Their parents both work long hours in pressured jobs in the media but try to do some home-working so that they can have more involvement with and oversight of their teenagers. Family relationships are generally positive and life is ordered – shopping, meals, housework and laundry are all planned and done in a routine manner. Every weekend there is a rota of jobs to be done that is allocated to each member of the family, such as cleaning, washing the car, cutting the lawn and walking the dog. However, the father always gets to walk the dog and takes the car to the car wash as his input. Jane plays her part perfectly but Karl falls far short. He is a bright, popular and energetic teenager but, as his dad says, 'is a complete slob'. He is also a star footballer and captains both his school year and his local boys' football teams.

The parents have tried a number of strategies for bringing him into line such as:

1. Rewards of extra pocket money

2. Grounding – withdrawal of freedoms to go out with friends at weekends and one school night a week until 9.30pm

3. Social withdrawal – making Karl eat on his own in the kitchen when the family have their usual Friday night meal on trays in front of the TV.

None of the above worked and have instead resulted in some emotional situations in which Karl and his father have become very angry with each other and on one occasion actually had a brief physical tussle.

The above situation is a very common one, and is unlikely to be shared with the school if, as in the case of Karl, the student is doing well. However, his room has become so squalid and disorganized that on several occasions he could not find school books containing completed homework that was due to be handed in and missed the deadlines. His form tutor, who enjoyed a good relationship with Karl and experienced him as a helpful and active member of the school community, asked him to stay behind after school in order to try to discover what was going on and to try to help. He found out that Karl was resentful of his parents' high regard and praise for his 'goody-two-shoes' sister, was unhappy about having so little time to mix with his friends and wanted to choose to eat on his own sometimes rather than with his family every single night. In addition, he said he would like to walk the dog sometimes but added with a laugh that he knew that his dad always did it as a way of getting out of other jobs at home. After talking with Karl his tutor asked for a consultation with the school's EP.

So what is going on here and what is there to work with?

The essence of Karl's situation is:

- Karl has a younger sister who he gets on well with even though she tends to be viewed as the ideal child by the parents

- Both parents work long hours, but they also do home-working to be available to their children

- Family life is ordered

- Each member of the family has designated chores and there are high expectations for standards of tidiness and order

- Karl and his father have been falling out often, and both mother and father have tried a number of strategies, positive and negative, for managing the situation and are keen to find one that works

- The school is keen to support Karl and his family and has been proactive in trying to help.

- What ideas do you have for helping Karl and his family to have a happier home life?
- What rules and choices operate in your day-to-day family life with respect to chores?

Esma, a sixteen year old who wants to decide her own dress code

Esma's parents have always been proud of her originality and interest in clothes, especially as they are quite reserved and traditional parents who are very careful to shield their children from exposure to the media and popular culture. However, as Esma's teenage years have progressed her parents have become more and more concerned about the sexualized way in which she has chosen to dress – very short skirts and low tops in bright, eye-catching colours and large amounts of make-up. They are also concerned about the example she is setting to her ten-year-old twin sisters. They understand that she needs to express her personality and have some choice in what she wears but she regularly, in their eyes, goes too far. Esma attends an all-girls' church school, which has a strict and rather old-fashioned uniform, which, by and large, Esma observes.

Things came to a head recently when the family attended church and Esma expected to be able to wear a pair of five-inch heels, fishnet tights, small denim shorts and a vest. Esma's father put his foot down and insisted she stay at home and as a result the wider family criticized him and his wife for allowing their daughter's church attendance to slip. Since then Esma has not been speaking to her mother and sometimes withdraws from the family completely, refusing to eat with them and spending periods alone in her room, coming home late from school more frequently via the local shopping centre with friends and picking on her sisters. Esma's aunt, who is close to Esma and her family, works for a local child and family adolescent service and she spoke in a general sense, i.e. did not identify anyone, with an EP about her sister and brother-in-law's worries.

So what is going on here and what is there to work with to help Esma and her family?

A summary of Esma's situation is:

- Esma is a confident and creative sixteen year old who wants to develop her own unique dress style and appearance

- Esma's parents have strong traditional values and as a result want to protect their children from exposure to the media and popular culture

- The parents are aware of the influence of Esma, their oldest child, on her younger siblings and are keen for her to set a positive example

- Esma attends an all-girls' church school, which has a strict and traditional uniform, with which she largely conforms

- Esma has a strong and positive relationship with an aunt, who is keen to be supportive of her niece and wants to help mend her family relationships.

- What ideas do you have for helping Esma and her family?
- What do you think teenagers should be able to choose with respect to their appearance?

My perspectives on Karl's and Esma's situations

Once more I make links with the seven models of adolescent development outlined at the end of Section 1, and have italicized key points in relation to the case studies.

Karl is clearly a resourceful young person and he is doing his best to make his life work and to do right by himself. In my experience this is the case for the vast majority of teenagers. The only problem is that he is not fulfilling his parents' expectations regarding contributing to the household chores and this has become an issue that has resulted in some nasty arguments and a bad atmosphere at home. If we take Erikson's model of adolescent development as a basis for understanding Karl it would be useful to explore what he thinks about his *identity*, i.e. how he sees himself in his different contexts – at home, at school and in the local community – and to notice any differences at play. In Karl's case he thought he was helpful at school and with his football clubs because he had chosen to be so, whereas at home he just saw the constant demands to help as being about his parents wanting to 'be the boss of him'.

Karl is developing *moral judgement* facilities (Kohlberg) and actively exercising some personal choice about what is right and wrong, so in some ways is in the final stage of development – *autonomous*. However, this is not working well for him and his family. I think his 'joke' about his dad getting to walk the dog as a way out of doing the chores is a clue as to how he views the privileges of being an adult male in the family, and in a way his refusal to toe the line is a communication that he is judging his father's behaviour and taking his cue from him. This identification with his father ties in with the model proposed by Blos and it follows that any meaningful change will require Karl to separate from the identification with his father, be critical of the position of non-helping that he has assumed and to develop his own separate sense of self and personal choices.

Drawing upon Bronfenbrenner's *process–person–context model*, which links with Bandura's ideas, the EP encouraged the form tutor to call a meeting with Karl and his parents and so bring together some of the different microsystems in which Karl operated. In an ideal world perhaps some of his friends and even the boys' community football coach might also be involved. The EP also emphasized the need to start the meeting by acknowledging the many helpful and positive aspects of Karl's behaviour at school and with his football clubs and to try to encourage Karl to share his views about choice and control. Hopefully from that point the parents and he could look more dispassionately at what was needed at home, give Karl more choice about which chores he helped with and to make sure that dog walking could sometimes be one of these. The meeting took place and was very positive. Hopefully in the long term Karl and his family found their own resolutions, as is the case for most general problems of adolescence over time.

Here is an acronym, which sums up a few of my suggestions on handling the need for control and choice around the house with teenagers:

How can you camouflage your wish for help with chores in such a way that your teenager gets to choose what they do and how they do them?

One area where you definitely need to loosen your own control agenda is the young person's room

Unless there is a health and safety issue, don't enter the teenager's room uninvited. Only do so if they invite you in

Set 'bottom-line' ground rules, such as their bedroom door stays shut if they choose to let it become a mess; clothes have to be put in the laundry basket if they want them washed and the room must be cleaned at least once a month

Esteem comes from a sense of belonging, achievement and having some control – don't make household chores be just about your control. Have relaxed conversations about '*our home*' and the good feelings and ease of living when it is in good order

Have an ongoing 'to do' list for jobs around the house and garden, e.g. tidying, hoovering, doing the laundry, emptying the dishwasher, cutting grass, feeding and walking pets, and make a column next to these where whoever does it adds their initials and dates

Once a week make a point of reviewing what has been done and who has done what – treats and rewards can be awarded in proportion to this. However, see my point about micro-managing below

Let go of perfectionism regarding the order and cleanliness of your home and set minimal standards

Develop a matter-of-fact, even relaxed, attitude to the day-to-day business of keeping the home going, as everything in time will get done

Choice is key to engaging adolescents in the life and maintenance of the household

However hard you try, you will not control your adolescent's behaviour as it is not yours but *their* job to ...

Own their behaviour and make the choices that affect them

Resist trying to micro-manage every aspect of your teenager's life as nothing disempowers people as much as this form of control exerted by others in power over them

Enjoy and expect to be surprised by what your teenager can contribute

Share your pleasure at such times and don't always think a material reward is necessary. You are still hugely important to your growing son or daughter and pleasing you and making you proud is generally their most cherished reward.

In some ways Esma's behaviour makes sense when viewed *eco-systemically* (Bronfenbrenner). After all, we live in societies in which vast importance is placed upon female appearance and attractiveness to the opposite sex. However, context is everything and as Esma is a bright girl who understands the different contexts of church, her social life, school etc., she is unlikely to have made her dress choices unwittingly. She is almost certainly making a statement about herself and the *identity* (Kohlberg) she has chosen, but she is also in a stage of *identity/role confusion* (Erikson), so is trying out different ways of dressing and experimenting with how she looks and the effect upon others.

Kohlberg's ideas about the adolescent development of moral reasoning are also useful. Esma is making a bid for her own choices and is clearly past the pre-moral stage of the very young child driven by expectations of personal reward or fear of punishment, and to some extent the conventional moral stage where she is actively testing the authority of adults. Her wish to dress exactly how she pleases regardless of context and situation is a sign of a young person who is striving for the mature autonomous stage where the individual exercises their own personal choice about what is right and wrong.

Bandura's *social-cognitive model* of adolescent development is certainly demonstrated in that Esma is actively making meaning of her social context in interaction with others. There is also scope for Blos' ideas about young people engaging in competition with or even defeat of their same-sex parent as Esma's mother's style of appearance couldn't be more different from the way her daughter wants to appear.

The advice Esma's aunt received from her EP colleague was for the parents and particularly the mother to try to have more conversations about how people dressed and presented themselves with Esma. This might be alongside some mutual TV and film watching or looking at magazines. She also suggested that the aunt who enjoyed a close relationship with her sister and niece might be a part of this, and make it a special older female activity that gave Esma a separate space/role from her younger siblings. She commented that Esma was fortunate to have another trusted adult in her life as the seemingly intense dynamics between mother and oldest daughter could be diluted through the aunt being more directly and positively involved and making a bridge between them.

Here is an acronym which sums up a few of my suggestions on handling teenagers' desires to have control and choice over how they dress:

Don't tell adolescents to do as you say but not as you do. Your choices for dress …

Reflect how you see yourself and not necessarily how your parents see you and it is the same for …

Each young person whose need and wish to be their own unique self is paramount

Show an interest in your adolescent's appearance along with other important areas such as their interests, their ideas and their views

Step back when you can and allow them to experiment and make mistakes from which they will learn profound lessons

Compromise where you can so that situations where a more relaxed dress code is appropriate can be times for the teenager to dress as they choose

Only set minimum rules such as the need for hygiene, cleanliness and decency

Don't expect teenagers to thank you for choosing and buying their clothes. Consider the possibility of a realistic clothing allowance – one that is feasible for your budget and one that is not so generous that they have no motivation for getting part-time, pocket-money jobs when the time is appropriate

Explain and discuss the need to be mindful of the situation and context so that they dress in a way that makes their lives easier and they avoid unnecessary conflict or sometimes even ridicule or disdain.

Summing up

All of the case studies in this and the preceding two chapters have been written to illustrate the particular core areas of motivation or need for teenagers – achievement, belonging and control/choice. In real life an educational psychologist's case work is rarely so clear-cut and is nearly always multi-factored and relates to more than one key need or issue. However, I know from my own experience of real-life day-to-day parenting of adolescents that thinking about these headings can be useful and can act as signposts while you travel the long journey of adolescence together.

Section 3:
Every unhappy teenager is different: areas of particular challenge

9. Becoming a teenager

The markers: physical, cognitive, social and emotional

I've already written about the wider social and historical context for being a teenager today, but now the focus will be on the basic and important changes and developmental processes that each young person must go through in order to mature into an adult. Psychologists and other professionals from medical and health settings often organize their assessments and interventions/treatments and individual programmes for young people according to the headings that I have used below, but must always be mindful of the fact that learning, growth and acquisition of particular skills have an effect on the young person's overall development and are happening in different areas simultaneously and at different rates. For example, a teenager might have achieved certain physical developmental milestones and appear to be approaching adulthood, but still be at a relatively immature level in terms of their emotional and social development, e.g. making unsound decisions about lifestyle and relationships and having little regard for the guidance of adults in their lives.

Physical

The physical changes that become evident during the teenage years are triggered by hormonal developments that begin much earlier during childhood. The two adrenal glands, which are located above the kidneys, become particularly active and trigger a physical process called 'adrenarche', which starts at about seven years of age for girls and about nine years of age for boys and continues through to the twenties. This starts the period of puberty. Early puberty is more common in girls and delayed onset of puberty more common in boys. Adrenarche involves the production of a 'sex hormone' called dehydroepiandrosterone (DHEA), and although scientists are not completely sure of its effects they think that it is responsible for accelerated skin gland secretion, the initially sparse growth of pubic hair and also the deposit of body fat. This, like all complex physical processes, is part of a series of other changes and processes and is thought to trigger full puberty. As children reach ten years of age and the start of the teens the pituitary gland becomes more active, producing a hormone called gonadotrophin, which, interestingly, happens at first mainly at night and causes the ovaries in girls and testicles in boys to produce sex hormones. Most accounts of physical changes in teenagers are organized in terms of those specific to girls and those specific to boys, so I will start by listing the changes common to *both sexes*:

- Increased skin secretions resulting in the appearance of spots, blackheads and sometimes acne. Also increased body odours

- Maturation of reproductive organs

- Increased growth of bodily hair, particularly noticeable in the axilla (armpits), genital area and on limbs

- Increased stature and weight, which can result in usually temporary awkwardness and self-consciousness

- Increased physical capacity, strength and competence

- Sensory strengths and preferences become more evident, e.g. a child with very acute hearing and musicality may demonstrate this through their musical development and performance.

Changes specific to *girls* include:

- Development of breast buds from as early as eight years. On average, breasts develop fully between twelve and eighteen years of age

- The beginning of menstruation, menarche, usually about two years after early breast development and appearance of pubic hair. The average range is between nine and sixteen years of age but there is a lot of individual variation

- Pubic, axilla and leg hair growth usually from nine to ten years of age, reaching adult patterns by thirteen or fourteen years of age

- General increased growth – the rate of increases in height and weight peaks on average at about eleven and a half years and slows down by about sixteen years.

Changes specific to *boys* include:

- Growth of testicles and scrotum from nine years of age although there is great individual variation. Full adult proportions are usually achieved by seventeen to eighteen years of age and at the same time the male voice gradually deepens

- Growth of pubic, axilla, chest and facial hair begins on average at about twelve years of age and reaches adult rates at about seventeen or eighteen years of age

- Experience of nocturnal ejaculations known as 'wet dreams' at the beginning of puberty – between thirteen to seventeen years of age

- General increased growth – the rate at which height and weight increases peaks on average at about thirteen and a half years and slows down by about eighteen years.

Cognitive

As I wrote in Chapter 4 cognitive theory is concerned with perception, thinking, learning and problem-solving. During the teenage years young people develop an increased capacity to think in abstract and 'bigger picture' ways, in relation to political, philosophical and social issues; to organize and plan; and to set longer-term goals, and as always there is great variation between individuals. They are also likely to think comparatively, for example about their own achievements, acquisitions, attributions, failures and challenges relative to peers.

In general, the formal education system around the world is organized to cater for the different cognitive developmental stages and related needs of teenagers, and most children make the transition from their first phase of education in Britain and many other parts of the world, known as the primary stage, to secondary education or high school. The curriculum, methods of teaching, arrangements for learning and assessment for teenagers' education all reflect the fact that students are generally capable of remembering information, i.e. have greater long-term memory capacities. Alongside this they are able to take in, understand, organize and apply information of an increasingly abstract nature. They are no longer at a developmental stage in which largely immediate, ideally concrete and personally relevant information is required. On top of all this teenagers are becoming more knowledgeable about learning itself and their own learning preferences, for example they will be increasingly capable of developing ways of retaining information through repetition and rehearsal, methods of organization and presentation such as imagery.

Social

Teenagers' quest for identity, control and choice, and independence and their role confusion – having recently been dependent children but being not yet adults – means that they usually challenge their parents to some degree or another. The social arena is one in which many of these challenges are very commonly evident. Here are a few of the issues surrounding the social development of teenagers that parents have shared with me:

- Teenagers can be heavily influenced by their peers, and often base their behavioural choices upon the approval and acceptance of friends. This may even include risky and/or illegal behaviours and activities

- Romantic/sexual relationships start to develop and to become important

- Teenagers can make such strong and long-term relationship commitments that other aspects of their life (studies, aspirations, family relationships and even health) suffer

- Teenagers can experience feelings of omnipotence – 'it won't happen to me' thinking – to the extent that they engage in risky behaviours and actions despite being conscious that these may result in unwanted consequences such as becoming pregnant, acquiring a sexually transmitted disease, driving or behaving recklessly or even illegally while under the influence of alcohol or drugs

- Teenagers can become involved in very closed gangs or cliques, which are characterized by dress/appearance codes, common behaviours and attitudes, and participation in certain activities. Some may even engage in secret rituals and use secret styles of communication.

This is generally more evident in the earlier stages of adolescence

- Teenagers are typically very self-absorbed, to the degree that they can believe they are the centre of everyone else's attention and this can mean they are hyper-sensitive to comments from others about their appearance or actions, which can lead to high emotion and conflictual situations.

Emotional

In Chapter 17 I focus particularly upon the emotional development and the heightened and sometimes difficult emotional experience of most teenagers, but of course as for all areas of teenage development there is huge variation. It would not be accurate to say that all teenagers experience marked highs and lows and are very emotional, but many are. The factors and processes that may trigger emotional outbursts are many, but there are several aspects of the teenage years that are consistent to all:

- They have to grow, quite literally, into a new physical form – one that is bigger, taller and more sexual

- They are becoming more aware of themselves as individuals and are striving to forge their own unique identities, which will involve comparisons with others, some positive and some negative. It is also likely to make them more self-conscious

- They are having to make increasing numbers of independent choices and decisions and to *be* consciously independent of their parents

- Their growing freedom and striving for independence means that they are experiencing more of the world and have the opportunity to make more choices. This can be confusing, frightening and overwhelming

- Their relative lack of life experience and their still immature neurological development, especially in the frontal lobe of the brain, which is where high-level, complex decision making, judgement, processing, organizing and applying of information processes take place, all add to the common emotional roller-coaster experience of being a teenager.

Why the teenage years are so much about change

- Physical changes affect the skin, reproductive organs, hair, stature, weight, physical capacity, sensory capacities and body odour
- Cognitive changes affect perception and thinking, including comparison with others, learning and problem-solving
- Social changes affect how teenagers see themselves, especially with regard to how they think others see

them, their perceptions of others and the value they place upon others in relation to themselves, their behavioural choices, their judgement, their priorities and their attachments

- Emotional changes affect the individual teenager's experience and expression of feelings, their management of difficult feelings and their sensitivity to the feelings of others.

10. Communication

Given the common perception of the teenage years is that this stage is one of conflict and high emotion, communication is an important topic. However, another widely held belief is that there is a *lack* of communication between teenagers and their parents. It is therefore appropriate that a chapter is devoted to this subject, and particularly to how to communicate as effectively and constructively as possible. I draw heavily upon the work of Virginia Satir (1916–88), who was originally a teacher and then became a psychotherapist, often referred to as a psychologist, and who is often viewed as the pioneer of family therapy. She very much belongs in a book that is drawing heavily upon positive and humanist psychology, as her underpinning beliefs, methods and writings illustrate. She believed and recognized that:

- The problems of an individual extend *to* the family and often stem *from* the family and therefore pathologizing individual family members was unhelpful

- People possessed the necessary mental health resources for their needs and professional support should facilitate their recognizing and using these

- Individual self-worth was key to effecting positive change and growth and intrinsic to healthy and helpful communication

- Physical methods such as breathing techniques, meditation, visualization and positive affirmation could help individuals engage with and use their resources and situations and achieve peace of mind

- Functional and healthy families and individuals experienced high levels of self-worth, communicated in specific, direct, clear and honest ways, had flexible, humane, appropriate rule systems and were open and hopeful about their place and role in society.

What is communication?

Most dictionary definitions define communication as the transfer of information between individuals through a common system of symbols, signs, sounds and/or behaviour. Other terms that feature in these definitions are rapport, message, instruction and connection. Virginia Satir wrote:

> *Communication is the largest single factor determining what kind of relationships she or he makes with others and what happens to each in the world.*
> Virginia Satir, *The New Peoplemaking* (1998)

The word communication comes from late Middle English and derives from Old French *comunicacion* and the Latin noun *communicationis* and the verb *communicare*, 'to share'. When we refer to communication this embraces not only spoken words, articulation, intonation and volume but facial expression, gesture, posture, breathing, proximity and actions. Many communication theorists state that only a small proportion, less than 10 per cent of what is communicated, is directly attributable to the actual words. However, it is undoubtedly the case that words can be very powerful and in some cases in a way that is unsupportive of, or may even block, communication. Virginia Satir offers this list of words that very much fall into this category and are ideally only used genuinely, with great care and in a loving way:

I, You, They, It, But, Yes, No, Always, Never, Should

All of these terms can be viewed as rather definitive and/or negative and therefore are not likely to open the way for discussion, sharing of views or resolving differences.

 Think about a conversation that you had recently with your teenager and try to recall the exact words that you used. You may find this difficult as most people forget very quickly the specific content of everyday conversations. Note if any of the words above were used and then decide:

- Did you use **I** in a useful way that made clear you owned what you were saying?
- Was **you** used in an accusatory way?
- Were **they** and/or **it** used clearly and specifically?
- If you used **but** was it helpful or confusing, and might you have more usefully used **and**?

- Did the words **always** or **never** feature, and were they helpful in working towards a solution?
- Were **yes**, **no** or **should** used, and if so were they used at the right time and in the right way for sorting things out?

The most basic of human needs are contingent upon our capacity to communicate, such as managing our core needs for survival; the development of friendships and intimacy; our productivity; and how we make sense of ourselves *and* the world and *in* the world. The vast majority of people have developed their communication capacities from birth and possibly even while in the womb, as some researchers of neonatal development believe. As humans we come 'primed' for language development and the complexity of brain structures and processes supporting this is a field of highly specialist enquiry and practice in itself. One idea that is widely understood, however, is that communication is learnt, from experience, from direct teaching and from the examples provided by others. This being the case, if young people can learn how to communicate better then there is every chance their relationships will improve. This makes it especially important that significant adults in teenagers' lives should set good examples of communication. Another hugely important idea is that communication relates to the process *between* individuals, and that therefore there is a transmitter and a receiver. In other words, both talking and listening are key.

One of the main reasons that communication between parents and teenagers can be so difficult is that parents and teenagers can seem to want different things. The parent has to find an appropriate balance of care and control, always maintaining the former while at the same time loosening the control that was necessary when their teenagers were children. The teenager, on the other hand, needs and wants to be independent, to have more choice and power in their life but also requires guidance, support and care from their parents.

These seemingly, at times, conflicting needs and drives for care and control can lead to conflict between parent and teenager. In the worst-case scenario a situation can result that is summed up well in the first four lines of William Blake's famous poem about conflict, 'A Poison Tree':

> I was angry with my friend:
> I told my wrath, my wrath did end
> I was angry with my foe:
> I told it not, my wrath did grow.

> William Blake, 'A Poison Tree' (1794)

In my work I have observed that nearly every conflict can be resolved or at least reduced and managed when better communication can be established. In families it is almost always the case that the conflict is only possible because there is such a deep connection between people and a level of trust or security exists that enables them to be as honest and emotional as they can be within a conflict. This very often means that young people and sometimes adults too can show their 'worst selves' – their most negative, aggressive and destructive behaviour.

The parent cannot make their teenager communicate well, but there is a lot they can do themselves such as communicating in specific, direct, clear and honest ways. Doing so is more likely to not exacerbate or even cause conflict, as well as providing a good example to their young people of how to go about preventing and/or managing conflict.

Unhelpful styles of communication

There are many unhelpful styles and patterns of communication and most probably we all experience different combinations of these daily, whether from ourselves or from others. Virginia Satir writes of four particularly unhelpful styles/patterns:

1. Placating
2. Blaming
3. Rationalizing, computer-like
4. Distracting.

The table below lists the kinds of words, body postures, gestures and feelings involved*:

---

* Strictly speaking, in a very literal sense, feelings are communicated through the first three columns – words, body posture and gestures. However, I have observed that individuals 'read' each other's emotional state (feelings) through not only these three means but also through an intuition or empathy. Hence my including it in this table.

Words	Body posture	Gestures	Feelings
Placating			
Generally pleasing, ingratiating, grateful, apologizing and never disagreeing.	A one-down way of carrying oneself; submissive; making oneself smaller and unthreatening; weak; uncertain; wobbly; hunched shoulders; arms helpless.	Lots of open palm gestures, nodding, metaphorically down on one knee.	'I feel like nothing.' 'I am here to affirm and be grateful to others, cause no trouble or never put myself first.'
Voice tends to be weak, low, perhaps whiny and squeaking.			
Blaming			
Negatively critical, attributing fault and weakness to others, e.g. 'You never ...', 'You always ...'.	Suggests 'I am more important than you', 'I know more than you', 'I am better than you.'	Finger pointing and wagging, one hand on hip and other raised in blaming gesture.	'I believe the best line of defence is attack.' 'I am actually quite insecure, lonely and failing.'
Name-calling.	Tightness and rigidity of posture, taking up space, dominating.		'I need someone else's apology to make myself feel better, more right and stronger.'
Loud, tight, often shrill and threatening voice.	Tight, rapid breathing; tight throat muscles; bulging eyes; flared nostrils; reddened skin.		
One-way communication.			

(continued)

Words	Body posture	Gestures	Feelings
Rationalizing, computer-like			
Ultra-reasonable, logical, rational, unemotional. Facts, numbers, statistics. Use of long, technical and abstract words. Paced, careful way of speaking.	Neutral, giving nothing away, unemotional, not terribly alive, certainly not warm. A rigidity, as though the skeleton is made of some inflexible metallic material. Mouth moves as little as possible, little facial expression.	Little gesture and movement. An upright and still style unmoved by feelings.	'I am not giving anything of myself away here, least of all my emotional state.' 'I am focused upon saying the right words and not showing how I feel as I actually feel quite vulnerable.'
Distracting			
The words are irrelevant to the time, place and situation. They make no sense and are rather 'off-piste'. The voice can be somewhat out of tune with the words, the intonation not appropriate to the words expressed. Rapid, breathless speech.	Angular, lacking in cohesion, off-balance, lots of rapid and uncoordinated movement.	Many awkward, irrelevant gestures, fast-moving arms, hands and mouth.	A feeling of being out of control, dizzy, confused. 'Where should I be?' 'What should I be doing and saying?' Focused upon anticipating the other's questions and points and rushing in without listening.

THINK ABOUT IT

Spot the unhelpful communication style/ pattern at play

Here are some made-up but hopefully recognizable situations between parents and their teenage children. Decide which of the following styles are evident in the parents' words:

1. Placating
2. Blaming
3. Rationalizing, computer-like
4. Distracting.

Bill, aged thirteen years
Bill has just had a major falling out with his best friend over a game of tennis and comes home much earlier than expected, red-eyed and puffy-faced. His dad Steve, who got a call from the tennis coach, says:

'You look like you lost a tenner and found 50p! Come on, son, man up! Isn't it a beautiful day?'

Most likely parental communication style/pattern?

Lola, aged sixteen years
Lola has been screaming and shouting into her mobile at the bottom of the garden and the neighbour has complained. When she comes in her mum says:

'I've decided to buy you those trainers you asked for and by the way, I'm making your favourite dinner. Why don't you go and watch TV, you can choose the programme tonight. Don't worry about the quiz show Dad likes.'

Most likely parental communication style/pattern?

Brendon, aged fifteen years
Brendon's twenty-year-old brother has found that a new pair of his trainers have been worn and scuffed. He reports this to the mum, who finds Brendon in his room and tells him:

'You are a selfish, dishonest boy who has no respect for other people's property. You will apologize to your brother and tell him that your pocket money for the next month will be used to buy him a replacement pair.'

Most likely parental communication style/pattern?

Nadia, aged seventeen years
Nadia's parents are both solicitors and have a large and beautiful home. Their domestic standards are extremely high and definitely more exacting than Nadia's, who has a habit of leaving her coat, bag and schoolbooks, among other things, lying around in the living and dining rooms. She also tends to leave dirty cups and dishes on the kitchen sink rather than putting them in the dishwasher after rinsing them. Nadia's mum has insisted that her father speak to her, so he goes to her room and states:

'Your mother and I have been evaluating how efficiently we all look after the house. I would appreciate any comments you would like to make about your contribution.'

Most likely parental communication style/pattern?

What is the most likely parental communication style/pattern being used in Nadia's example?

It is quite hard to identify clear communication styles/patterns when all you have to go on is a situation and the words that were used. This illustrates the point that communication involves so much more. Putting the facts of each situation to one side, what else would you expect in order to be more sure about the style/pattern of communication being used by Nadia's parent? Think about bodily posture, gestures, the parental feelings involved.

You might like to consciously try using these four communication styles, i.e. role-play them in an exaggerated, fun way. Perhaps you will prefer to do it with another adult but it would also be extremely useful to involve your teenager. Everyone needs to be aware of, learn about and continually try to improve their own particular way of communicating.

Here's an acronym which sums up some useful things to remember about communicating well with your teenager:

Choices and compromise rather than commands and instruction help a great deal

Occasionally do the unexpected. If your teenager has got into the habit of having tantrums and shouting matches try covering your ears, lie on the floor, sit unresponsively and wait out the storm or maybe leave the room and write a note or a text

Make what you as parent find acceptable and unacceptable clear and model this. This includes bad language, name-calling and rudeness, including that which might be directed at yourself by your son or daughter. It is important to make clear your own right to maintaining self-worth and self-respect

Make your values clear and your rules as minimal as possible and confined to absolute musts and must-nots, e.g. health and safety issues, but once decided hold the line

Ultimatums and heavy sanctions generally don't work over time. You need to be able to work together with your teenager so that they internalize what is right/wrong, acceptable/unacceptable, safe/unsafe – they should take on board the reasoning and value of such beliefs

Never make a performance out of a conflict with a teenager. Take the disagreement away from others who are not involved in a helpful way

Instead of dismissing or ignoring feelings acknowledge with a word or words, sound and/or gesture and offer the chance to talk it through

Control your own emotions and remember that as the adult it is important to manage and demonstrate this skill

Attempt to keep communication going and never withdraw the opportunity for your teenager to talk with you. When your teenager gives you the cold shoulder and won't talk with you, if there is another involved and responsible adult with whom the teenager can relate and communicate well, encourage them to talk with the young person and to act as a bridge between you and your teen

Time and timing are key. Sometimes a cooling-off period, an opportunity and a space to process and think, is beneficial to both parent and teenager

Expectations and wishes need to be expressed and clarified, both yours and the young person's

What you are feeling does matter and there is every benefit in expressing this as long as you can be an example of mature and calm emotional management

Express appreciation through describing the behaviour that has pleased you and remember the rule of thumb to make three positive comments to each one that is not. It is generally best to give praise for observable behaviour rather than the person as a whole

Logic and rationality can be unhelpful for some highly charged emotional and/or relationship issues and situations

Love is the driving force behind most parent/teenager conflicts but sometimes becomes lost or forgotten. Hard as it is when provoked and challenged, try to remember the small child or even infant your son or daughter used to be and that is still somewhere in both yours and your teenager's memory and thinking.

One last point to remember is that seeming non-communication, usually characterized by silence and with-drawal, the classic sulk, is still a type of communication and a very powerful one at that. As a parent it is important to resist this and when a teenager engages in this to *keep trying* to help them to communicate overtly in a healthy and effective way. In other words, keep the door open to working things out by resisting the urge to be angry, frustrated or compliant in this non-communication.

11. Family relationships

The relationships we have with our parents, siblings and extended family are life long. Whether or not contact is maintained later in life, and in most cases it is, the connections or lost connections have an emotional significance and meaning that is with us for life, and which acts as a foundation for our development and learning and contributes to our overall well-being. Of course, families are all different and not all are the traditional nuclear setup of mother, father and two-plus children, and even if they are, the emotional undercurrents, tensions and family scripts still vary hugely. When a family involves second or more marriages, stepparents and siblings and new extended family members the situation is, by definition, even more complex. The fact that family structures and compositions are changing is another factor that means it is not possible or wise to be prescriptive about how difficulties should be addressed, but family therapist Virginia Satir's ideas about what makes for a functional and healthy family continue to be useful – the individuals within them have high levels of self-worth, communicate in specific, direct, clear and honest ways, have flexible, humane, appropriate rule systems and are open and hopeful about their place and role in society. That last point regarding a family's relationship to the wider society is reflected in both the changing profile and nature of families and in their need to be creative, positive and resourceful in finding and using solutions for their own unique problems and issues.

 According to Virginia Satir the components and characteristics of a healthy and functional family include:

- Members who value and feel positive about themselves
- Members who communicate well; that is, they are clear, direct, specific and honest in what they say to each other
- Family rules that are appropriate, kind and sensitive and, where necessary, flexible
- Members that are open and optimistic about their connection with and place in society.

Changing family structures

The Office for National Statistics' most recent labour force survey of 2017 states that in that year:

- There were 19 million families in the UK
- There were 12.9 million married or civil partner couple families in the UK. This was the most common type of family
- Cohabiting couple families were the fastest growing family type
- Married couple families include both opposite-sex and same-sex married couples. Cohabiting couple families

127

include both opposite-sex and same-sex cohabiting couples

- Young males were more likely to be living with their parents than young females; around 32 per cent of males aged twenty to 34 years were living with their parents compared with 20 per cent of females aged twenty to 34 years in 2017
- The number of families in the UK represented a 15 per cent increase from 16.6 million in 1996.

Reasons why family relationships are so important for teenagers

Families are where we make our first relationships, develop a sense of self and, very importantly, self-worth. Ideally it is through the learning about relationships and oneself that the child develops resilience, closeness with others and the tools for building, maintaining and managing relationships and how to live in the world in general.

Famous child development theorists such as John Bowlby, Mary Ainsworth and Donald Winnicott developed 'attachment theory', a fundamental idea of which is that children learn about relationships in a way that is internalized, i.e. serves as a template for all future relationships and the individual's relational style, which is characterized according to how they deal with attachment to others and also separation.

For reasons that have already been explored in previous chapters, particularly in Chapter 5, which presents a number of key theories of adolescent development, finding a unique identity, becoming independent and trying out different ways of being are core to being a teenager. This usually results in their testing the system of family relationships into which they have been born and in which they live, and particularly their parents who have to be sensitive to their young people's stage of development, actions, thoughts and beliefs, and need for experimentation and at the same time offer support and care. I have found ideas from family therapy extremely useful for understanding and working with those young people and their families who have come to me because of difficulties.

Family therapy ideas

Family therapy is a way of offering therapy to a whole family and it also presents a set of ideas, which are helpful for thinking about and supporting parents of teenagers in their parenting. Although there are a number of types of family therapies, the following ideas are common to all:

- Problems in families are viewed as repeating patterns in the interactions between family members, which result from and also maintain the underlying problem. In other words, problems in families are not just about one individual but are about what occurs *between* individuals
- These repeating patterns are usually ones which occur not only in the family of focus but also in past generations. They are inter-generational

- The family system includes the actions, relationships and underlying beliefs of the family, including past generations, over time
- The beliefs of the family are influenced by the reasons people live together; rules about life and how it should be lived; environmental factors (the economy, times of war/peace, social opportunities, accommodation possibilities) and cultural opinions and values (thoughts on different types of relationship, such as inter-racial and between different classes)
- In order to address problems in family systems therapists must identify, make explicit and address the reasons why the problem exists and continues
- Family therapists very often become involved when the family is undergoing major changes. The teenage years, by definition, represent major changes to the family system.

Here is a very simplified summary of a family who benefited from family therapy:

Gillian, an academically bright seventeen year old who wished to leave school as soon as she could and has had a series of unskilled jobs, behaves badly – she has been caught shoplifting, been absent from school, stayed out late getting drunk and she is viewed as the 'bad child' in her family. Gillian lives with her biological father and his second wife, her stepmother, and their fifteen-year-old son, Gillian's half-brother Gary. Gary can do no wrong and is often referred to as 'the angel child'.

The first thing the family therapist did when she met with the whole family was draw a map of the family called a genogram. This included names and ages, occupations, places of residence, marriages, separations, divorces, illnesses, deaths and other significant events of three generations of the family. In doing so she found that there was a pattern of female teenagers becoming disenfranchised from their families because of behaviour that got them into trouble, either being expelled from school, getting pregnant or committing criminal acts. This inevitably meant that the period of dependency upon the family continued long into adulthood. The male teenagers, on the other hand, were generally pro-social, did well at school and caused no difficulties. Gillian's stepmother was the first to recognize this pattern and related strongly to it as she became pregnant very early in her relationship with Gillian's father, when he was still married to Gillian's biological mother, when she (Gillian's stepmother) was only fifteen. Some interesting and emotional discussions took place about how it was to be a teenage girl in the family, the expectations of parents, relationships with male siblings and the various future options available. The breakthrough came when the stepmother told Gillian that she had always wanted to go to university and study medicine, which had been Gillian's aspiration during primary school and which she now decided to work towards again, with the help of her family.

THINK ABOUT IT
What do you think the underlying beliefs are in Gillian's family system?

Points to consider: sex of child, dependency, independence, pro-/anti-social behaviour.

....

....

....

Although you may not necessarily have marked problems and issues as in Gillian's example, it is a useful exercise to consider what *your* beliefs about teenagers, growing up, dependence and independence are. Perhaps jot down, very spontaneously, what immediately comes to mind and bear in mind that your ideas and the other parent's may well not be identical.

....

....

....

What sort of problems are commonly experienced in families with teenagers?

Family therapy has identified two major and common relationship issues, which are: *enmeshment* and *disengagement*. In reality most families feature a combination of, and an often temporary mixture of, enmeshed and disengaged relationships but whatever is happening in one part of the family system has an effect on other parts.

Enmeshment is a term used to describe relationships that are extremely close, frequently to the point that relationships external to the family system can be excluded. This is not necessarily a problem and can be entirely appropriate for a period of time, e.g. parents and a newborn child, when intimate relationships are being established and at times of bereavement. In a family with an enmeshed relational style there is typically a level of emotional connection that means:

- If one member of the family experiences emotional distress so does everyone else
- The response to even small amounts of emotional distress is fairly immediate
- Differences between individuals within the family system are discouraged and/or not supported
- Enmeshed families typically believe in 'one for all and all for one' and claim to be able to 'read each other's minds'.

Teenagers in families with an enmeshed style can find their families emotionally stifling and in their quest for an individual identity, independence and more choice/control in their own lives can be experienced as disruptive, challenging and destructive of the family's general ethos and culture.

Disengagement is a term used to describe distant and uninvolved relationships and dynamics in a family. In a family with a disengaged relational style there is typically a level of emotional disconnection that means:

- Everyone is encouraged to stand on their own two feet
- Individuality and difference are highly valued and encouraged
- A lack of awareness and response to the emotional issues, actions or changes that may be affecting individuals in the family
- Difficulties with communication of feelings and even discouragement of such expression.

Teenagers in a family with a disengaged relational style may be so determined to go their own way and do things independently that they are not given the opportunity to seek help and/or receive emotional support. Sometimes, in extreme cases, their behaviour may be anti-social and/or dangerous and this can be experienced as 'acting out' and attention-seeking by others in the family. It might also be viewed as a 'cry for help'.

Dryads – two-person alliances such as mother and father and relationships between siblings of the same sex or similar age; triads – three-person alliances; and hierarchies – power-based relationships – are also of special interest to family therapists, as they reveal so much about what is going on within the family and how they might be helped to understand its core and often unhelpful beliefs, and overcome its problems and issues.

Here is an acronym that sums up some ideas that are helpful in solving family relationship problems:

Family relationships are not fixed in time and nature and can be improved

All members of the family are a part of both problems and solutions

Members of a family are defined by the emotional connections, both positive and negative, that each person feels in their own way

Ideal families share humour, affection, emotions and love

Let differences and conflict be expressed constructively and with respect. Use them as an opportunity for growth

Yesterday, today and tomorrow merge over and over again in every family over time

Resolution of differences may mean compromise and/or concession and always involves communication

Every family has issues and problems to address

Let each individual child *be* individual as well as a part of the family

Allow time and space for different relationships within the family

Try to make sure that each parent spends some time with each child

Individual time and space is important for everyone

Open up the family home to other people when you can

Never consciously typecast one child relative to the other/s. If you realize you are doing it unconsciously then question this

Sibling relationships are complex and complicated but enduring in the minds of all involved even if not in actuality

Have some times and activities for the family as a whole but accept that as children age they may sometimes opt out

Invite the views of all family members as much as possible in working towards solutions and resolutions

Praise and constructive criticism are usually best given to individual children one to one but sometimes it is appropriate to have a collective celebration or discussion as a whole family

Sharing, trusting, waiting and hoping are all high ideals not easily or always attained, but worth striving for.

 Think about a recent issue or problem to do with relationships in your own family and use this 'facts, feelings and wishes' approach, which is often used in schools for mediating conflictual situations:

- What are the *facts* of what happened? Can you think in objective and factual terms about the situation?

  ....

  ....

- What *feelings* did you experience, what *feelings* were expressed? Put into words the emotional experience that this situation created for you.

  ....

  ....

- What *wishes* do you have for working towards a resolution? In an ideal world, suspending disbelief and practicality for the time being, what would you like to

137

happen? Let your imagination roam and be as creative as you like.

....

....

Perhaps this exercise has given you some new perspectives and ideas about relationships in your family and the difficult situations and feelings that can exist? If so, note them down:

....

....

....

12. Peer relationships

The development of social skills

Even from the pre-school days of earliest childhood, children are developing ways of relating to and with other children of their age. The process of developing social skills is a long, gradual and sometimes recursive one. Their understanding of how to interact with others, friendship and friendly behaviour, conflict and conflict management develops over time and reflects the individual child's temperament, preferences and situation. Most parents are all too aware of the need to support and guide their children in this aspect of development but will also know that there is no 'one-size-fits-all' method or set of clear rules for doing this and that it can be emotionally challenging. Involved professionals know that other aspects of the child's development are part of this growing capacity to socialize, for example, their cognitive and language capacities, their development of moral reasoning and judgement skills and their sense of identity.

Research on children's peer relationships has identified some broad and approximate phases of development, which the majority of children reach and pass through as they mature and grow. From about two to four years of age the interest children have in each other and the wish to engage directly with them through play increases. The young child's growing language and cognitive and physical capacities all facilitate this, and the ability to play independently and in a relatively undirected way increases. Once children start formal education, which is about five years of age in the UK but does vary across the world up to about seven years, they begin to grasp the need for reciprocity, i.e. sharing and turn-taking when engaged in activities with peers. They also exercise more choice and experience preferences in relation to playmates and in who they do not want to play with. Their understanding and management of conflict and disagreement develops too, although it would be fair to say a certain amount of competition between children of this age is often apparent. Friendship pairings and groups form but do change quite a lot, as any primary teacher will testify. By about nine years of age friendships tend to become same sex, although as a visitor to numerous primary school playgrounds I can say this is not always or necessarily the case. The boys' groups are generally bigger and activity related whereas girls' groups are smaller and more 'conversational'. The complexity of play and collaborative activity increases.

Think back to when your teenager was first starting school and began to make friends. Think about the issues with which you had to help. Do you remember what you said or did to help your child? Share your memories with your teenager and ask if their memories are similar, especially those which they recall made a positive difference. If your teenager is experiencing particular difficulties with friends it may be more helpful to do this exercise in a more subtle way, by having the conversation about a younger member of the family or extended family and their early friendship challenges.

Social and emotional development in teens

As the teenage years begin peer relationships tend to be highly selective, very often in relation to perceived similarities such as race or ability, and relationships deepen so that personal disclosure, problem-sharing and the range and depth of discussion and disclosure increase. Young teens are more and more aware of the differences in perception, feeling and expectation between themselves and others. They are starting to value the individual qualities and characteristics of their friends rather than just what the other can do for or give to them. They will probably have a range of different kinds of friends but attribute their strongest relationships, to which they can be extremely committed and loyal, to their peers that have the power to support and affect them emotionally as well as practically. They will be more sensitive to the effect of their words and actions on others and as a result are usually more circumspect and reflective about what they do and say. Ideally, school and family environments should be tuned in to this, and adults actively modelling pro-social attitudes and behaviour. In the worst-case scenarios social exclusion or even bullying can occur as a result of this new awareness and development of social skills.

Why peer relationships are so important to teenagers

Sometimes the strength of teenagers' peer relationships as they move through the middle and later teenage years can cause parents and involved adults concern and the phenomenon of cliques and gangs is widely documented in literature, the arts and the media, very often in negative terms. Taking a positive psychology perspective, it is easy to see what the gains for teenagers are in identifying so strongly with their peers and wanting to spend increasing amounts of time with them. As I've written repeatedly throughout this book, the journey that teenagers have to make between childhood and adulthood is a challenging one and there is so much for them to learn, negotiate, understand and achieve. Other teenagers understand and recognize this, as they are on the same journey, and the urge to experiment and test is usually common to all. Relationships with peers are fundamental to the teenager's individual identity development, their capacity to live in harmony with others in a social context, their social understanding, communication skills and many emotional capacities. Even the most sensitive and constructive of parents cannot know from direct experience how it is to be a teenager at that particular time as they will have grown up in a different time, culture and social context. However, the availability of guidance, support and love from parents and other involved adults as and when the teenager wants it continues to be important, as it probably always will be.

Peer relationship problems

Most parents of teenagers will have been concerned about their teenager experiencing some of the following common problems:

- Issues to do with popularity
- Problems with making friends
- Loneliness
- Problems with maintaining friendships and friendships ending
- Arguments
- Bullying (this will be covered in Chapter 13).

Issues to do with popularity and what parents can do to help

The popular teenager is usually one who has developed a good level of social skills, including good communication skills and emotional awareness, and in addition has a positive self-regard and sense of self-worth. The preceding chapters on family relationships and communication offer some ideas about how to support this with your teenager. It is important to appreciate that popularity – being the individual that a larger than average number of peers want to interact and/or spend time with – may not necessarily indicate well-developed personal, emotional and social skills and qualities. Sometimes relatively superficial social skills such as making others feel important, flattered and special are at play, and these are not the ingredients for psychological health and well-being, as the many famous celebrities and high-achievers of our times who disclose unhappiness, relationship problems and mental health issues make evident. Healthy relationships are reciprocal, emotionally honest and constructive. When differences arise the individuals concerned can express these safely and find a way to compromise, recognize shortcomings and disappointments and agree a way forward.

It is important that parents share their own experiences and views on the subject of popularity with their teenagers in everyday conversation. The celebrity culture pervades our everyday media and arts, and so opportunities to start conversations about the popularity of individuals who fit this description are easily available. Watching television together, discussing newspaper and magazine articles and music are perfect opportunities for these discussions. The key idea that parents need to try to communicate on the subject of popularity is that it is the quality of rather than the quantity of friendships that matters.

Teenagers today have many social interactions that are conducted via new media where the complex and some-times delicate social processes described above don't nec-essarily take place and therefore their personal, social and emotional development can suffer. The whole commercial business of how many social media followers a person may have trades upon individuals' friendships and relationships and has worrying implications for mental health, emotional well-being and social connection. Research into this area is growing and the government and other organizations concerned about children and young people's well-being are offering advice and guidelines about how parents can influence their children's use of new technology. Some of the best places to find these are:

- The Children's Society – see 'Safety Net' report
- The National Society for the Prevention of Cruelty to Children (NSPCC)
- Young Minds
- The Department for Education (DfE) (2016 'Child Safety Online: A practical guide for parents and carers whose children are using social media', which draws upon Professor Tanya Byron's governmental review and the 2008 'Safer Children in a Digital World').

Dr Mariann Hardey of Durham University, interviewed on Radio 4's *Thinking Allowed* programme, described her research into the deliberate non-use of new technology. This idea, of consciously disconnecting from phones, computers and social media in general, could be a useful strategy for parents, as benefits appear to include more direct contact with others, more activity and generally feeling better and more present – less stressed, anxious and overloaded. If parents can set this example from time to time and, very importantly, engage their teenagers in conversations about this way of living, the benefits could be substantial.

Problems with making friends

Of all the common derogatory terms that teenagers use to describe peers one of the worst is 'loner', one that parents never like to hear about their own child. Others include 'weirdo', 'nerd' and 'loser', and suggest a young person who has few or even no friends. The desire to avoid these labels is probably one of the driving forces for teenagers so readily forming cliques, groups and gangs.

Most children reach their teenage years with some friendship-making skills. They learn from experience, and also from direct teaching and observation, and some children, probably some of those with a reputation for popularity, are particularly good at these skills. Sue Roffey, an educational psychologist and writer, has written an excellent book (with T. Tarrant and K. Majors), *Young Friends: Schools and Friendship* (see references), from which I will summarize some useful ideas about how you can help your teenager learn more about the skills of friendship-making. Individuals who make friends easily tend to:

- Exhibit friendly behaviour, which includes a tendency to communicate in a positive way through both words and non-verbal behaviour. They demonstrate acceptance of others, approach others appropriately, behave caringly, have a high awareness of their own feelings and can feel and express empathy

- Show through their movement, gesture, body position and facial expressions that they are approachable, friendly and positive
- Make the right amount of direct eye contact
- Have friendly facial expressions – smiling, warm and open
- Judge the appropriate distance/proximity to others – not too close or so far away that it is uncomfortable and awkward.

 Share the list above with your teenager at an appropriate time and have a conversation about the people they know who show friendliness and perhaps those who do not. There is no need to make this into a personal inventory of friendly characteristics for you and/or your teenager unless it seems appropriate and comfortable to do so. Most likely this will only be the case if it is your teenager that suggests you and/or they might do this.

Lots of the literature on friendship suggests that personal similarities, shared situations and/or activities and interests are good starting points for beginning a friendship. While you have less leeway to set up situations and activities where your teenager is well placed to make new friends than when they were younger, there are still possibilities, which may start through everyday conversations in which your teen may offer you the chance to start talking about this area. The important thing is that you do not give the impression that your teenager is somehow lacking or at fault for experiencing some difficulties with making friends. This is where being honest about your own experiences at their age can be helpful as long as you can talk positively about what you found useful and what worked for you. If you cannot, perhaps there is another involved adult who might help? Schools have become more aware of the need to actively support the social and emotional development of their pupils and although the direct and overt focus of the DfE's 2005 'Social and Emotional Aspects of Learning' (SEAL) programme is not as evident in education today, it is still worthwhile taking a look at the materials and approaches that schools were encouraged to use and this is available online on the National Archives website. At this time schools' personal, social and health curriculums contain material that relates to social and emotional development but as it is of a non-statutory nature it will vary from school to school, as will the importance afforded it.

Loneliness

Very closely allied to difficulties with making friends is the experience of feeling lonely but as one of the points in the acronym below summarizes, it is possible to still feel lonely even when you have friends or can make friends easily.

This acronym offers a way of thinking about the experience of loneliness so that it is easier to raise and discuss the subject with your teenager:

Loneliness is a perception or feeling that generally passes in time

Once you start to feel lonely it can be difficult to reason yourself out of that feeling

Numerous situations and happenings can trigger feelings of loneliness, for example: being bored; doing something wrong; being blamed; having an argument; losing someone; missing someone; failing or not being chosen; being embarrassed or ashamed

Everyone can feel lonely. It is a universal experience for people of all ages

Loneliness can be experienced when you are alone and also when you are with others, even large numbers of others

Individual and genuine concern from people who care about and like you, being with pets, doing activities, listening to music, watching films and reading books or other favourite activities can all help

Negative emotions are always involved in feeling lonely

Emotions to do with loneliness include: sadness; emptiness; feeling cold; feeling different or wrong in some way relative to others; feeling excluded and/or unwanted and/or worthless and/or uncared for and/or disconnected from others

Sometimes being alone and having solitude can be a happy and content time. Most people enjoy solitude sometimes as well as social times

School, home or being out and about can all be places where you can feel lonely.

 Think about yourself at the same age as your son or daughter is now. When and how did you feel lonely at that time? What helped? What made it worse?

Consider sharing your thoughts about your responses to the above with your child, and if they are willing to do so talk about *their* experience of feeling lonely. Make sure you finish with what helped you.

Problems with maintaining friendships and with friendships ending

Teenagers tend to form more lasting relationships than when they were younger and although the difficult and emotional experience of a friendship ending, for whatever reason, tends to be managed better and is often not talked about, parents can usually tell from their teenager's general demeanour, social activity and behaviour when there has been a breakup. Teenagers are actively exercising choice and are more aware of the sort of friends they want, so when they have problems with keeping friends most parents would like to be able to help. During conversations with your teenager try to share the idea that sometimes a friendship has simply run its course and although this may cause sadness and regret to some degree, which should be acknowledged, this will pass in time. It is also worth making the point that every experience, even, or maybe especially, the difficult and challenging ones, can be learnt from, so that the person is better equipped for future situations and events.

Keeping friends

All true friendships must be reciprocal and meet the needs, as much as possible, of both parties. Sometimes compromise is required, which means that one person may have to wait or forego what they would have liked to happen, but over time hopefully this levels out. Most people have various different friendships that serve some or all of these different functions:

- Having fun
- Doing activities together
- Sharing and developing interests
- A way of forming, supporting and/or confirming a distinct personal identity

- A sense of belonging and being wanted and valued as a friend
- A way of supporting understanding and learning about the world
- A way of supporting the development of communication and emotional and social capacities
- A way of accessing emotional and social support.

THINK ABOUT IT Think about your own friendships at this time and decide which of the above functions they serve for you. You might also think about which friendships you value the most and about how you have maintained them. The material you get from this exercise might be shared in a relaxed conversation with your teenager. You can also try the following quiz, either on your own or with your teenager, and then talk about your thoughts following it.

Quiz: What Kind of Friend Are You?
I have adapted this quiz from a book about adolescence, written by Elizabeth Fenwick and Dr Tony Smith (see references), into one that takes a positive psychology perspective – i.e. focuses upon the positive qualities, virtues and strengths of friends and your value as a friend.

		YES	MOSTLY OR OFTEN	NO
1	**Do you feel you are a friend worth having?** People who have good self-regard and self-worth are usually more comfortable to be with than those who do not.			
2	**Do you ask a reasonable amount of time, energy and attention from friends?** It is easier to have friends who can appreciate the other activities and people in your life and who are secure about what is available to them from you.			
3	**Are you loyal?** Can you be trusted to keep the confidences of friends? Can you be relied upon to support them when they need your backing and/or help?			
4	**Do you try to be positive about others as much as possible?** Do you try to say pleasant and affirmative things to your friends?			
5	**Do you sometimes make the first friendly move?** You need to sometimes be the person who makes the first gesture of friendliness or invitation to be a friend rather than wait for others to do this.			
6	**Do you take the initiative to offer help when it is needed?** Wanting to help and offering this is a highly valued quality in others.			

(continued)

153

		YES	MOSTLY OR OFTEN	NO
7	**Do you participate with enthusiasm and energy?** Sometimes you have to put yourself forward rather than responding to others' invitations and this is appreciated by others.			
8	**Are you friendly to others who seem to be excluded, whether through their own reticence or the active exclusion of others?** By showing empathy and interest in those who are clearly not part of the 'in-group' or the popular crowd you demonstrate some very desirable personal qualities in a friend.			
9	**How good a listener are you?** Listening is an important communication skill. It shows that you are not just interested in yourself and it makes others feel valued and generally good about themselves.			
10	**If someone looks unhappy would you show concern and/or try to cheer them?** Kindness costs very little and shows the warm heart that others want in friends.			
11	**Are you able to understand and be flexible when a friend has to change a plan that involves you?** Everyone's lives are complicated now and again and plans have to be adjusted. It is good to have friends who can cope with this.			
12	**Do you enjoy collaborating with others sometimes?** Doing and producing things with friends can be a source of great joy, learning and productivity.			

Answering yes to all of the above suggests you are a kind, empathic, fair, confident, active, positive, loyal, enthusiastic, interesting person who listens, cares and supports all the time. In other words, close to saintly! I included an additional response column, 'mostly/often', because in reality we don't always present our best selves to others or do what we know is right, but if we aspire to have and to use these qualities we are likely to have many good-quality friendships.

As well as supporting better awareness of their own qualities as a friend, this exercise is good for understanding what kind of friends the teenager wants. Parents can be very concerned about their teenage child's friendship choices, but at this stage the young person's choice has to be just that – their choice – and it is worth remembering that the friends *you* have may not be the ones that significant others in your life might choose. In the worst-case scenario they may actively dislike them, but their judgement is not based on your knowledge of that person, who is your friend. If you have worries about your teenager's friend or friends, one way to address this is to get to know them better by encouraging them to be brought home. Show an interest and try to be friendly, until you have reason not to be. It is important to not wade in immediately, making judgements and being critical. If you can keep positive communication going and find ways of talking generally about friendships and other things like lifestyle choices, school and appearance, health and safety, the teenager will make the friendship choices that are good for them and learn what they need to learn.

Arguments

If you think back to your own teenage peer relationships you may well recall those that ended with an argument and there are likely to be some that never recovered. The William Blake poem about conflict that I quoted from in the chapter about communication (Chapter 10) makes clear the need for clear and constructive communication in those relationships that are important to you and that you wish to continue. Chapter 10 also makes some suggestions for effective communication. As a parent you can hopefully set good examples of this and as the family is a relational structure and relationships by definition are going to feature the occasional disagreement, if not full-blown argument, there are likely to be opportunities to do so. Many parents tell me that their life with teenage children is a time of frequent argument, so again, plenty of opportunities to teach by example!

If your teenager asks you for help or simply to talk about a problem with friends, then let them lead the discussion and keep your questions open rather than closed, for example:

'What do you think the problem is?' is an open question.

'How did you make this problem happen?' is a closed question.

Be actively curious and constructive, for example: 'What have you tried so far and what has worked even a little bit?'

Encourage persistence, optimism and effort, for example: 'What could you try that may make a difference?'

Put arguing into context – let them know that it usually features in relationships, especially those that mean more to us, for example: 'Most people have arguments now and again, and it can be helpful for working out how to have a better relationship.'

13. Bullying

In the 1980s the British education system woke up to the fact that bullying happened in schools and the Department for Education responded to the advice of groups of professionals, the growing research base and the culture of disclosure of some very high-profile individuals' first-hand experiences with new educational legislation and guidance. Now, in Britain, as for many other parts of the world, all schools are required to have an anti-bullying statement within their whole-school behaviour policy and school staff are required to work in a way that addresses all potential and actual incidents of bullying, including:

> *Encouraging good behaviour and respect for others on the part of pupils and, in particular, preventing all forms of bullying among pupils.*
> Section 89 of the Education and
> Inspections Act, 2006

This provides a framework for what parents can do if they consider their child is being bullied.

Defining bullying
The three factors that distinguish bullying from other aversive behaviours are that bullying:

1. Usually takes place between two individuals of a similar age and there is often an additional group dynamic, where a bully has supportive and collusive allies.

2. Happens repeatedly over time. It is not a one-off conflict or aggressive act.

3. Takes place as a result of a power imbalance – either in terms of physical strength, academic ability or social status. Individual differences between bully and the bullied are such that it is difficult for the bullied person to defend themselves and they are therefore more vulnerable.

Impact of bullying

Current research into bullying between young people such as that undertaken by Professor Andrea Danese, who heads the Stress and Development Lab at the Social, Genetic and Developmental Psychiatry (SGDP) Centre, and the Department of Child and Adolescent Psychiatry, Institute of Psychiatry, Psychology and Neuroscience at Kings College London, provides evidence that bullying contributes to mental health problems which can have long-term effects right up to and during the adult years. Bullying affects a person's self-esteem, trust in the world, capacity to function, to achieve, to belong and to exercise some choice and control over themselves and their lives. Mental health issues affecting teenagers can arise from many situations and activities, which I touch on in other chapters, but it is useful at this point to consider what is meant by good mental health and well-being. The British Royal College of Psychiatry states that it results in:

A combination of feeling good and functioning effectively. The concept of feeling good incorporates positive feelings of happiness and contentment, and also interest, engagement, confidence and affection. The concept of functioning effectively (in a psychological sense) involves the development of one's full potential, having some control over one's life, having a sense of purpose such as working towards valued goals and experiencing positive relationships.

From 'Did you know?
Information briefing on well-being'
(Huppert, 2009)

The World Health Organization (2014) states:

Mental health is defined as a state of well-being in which every individual realizes his or her own potential, can cope with the normal stresses of life, can work productively and fruitfully, and is able to contribute to her or his community.*

---

*   http://www.who.int/features/factfiles/mental_health/en/

A useful checklist of warning signs that will help you know when to arrange help for your teenager

When a young person is experiencing bullying, some or even all of the following signs, which are actually common to other types of mental health difficulty, may be evident:

- **Difficulties** across all parts of the school day and reported difficulties out of school

- **Changes** in core behaviours, e.g. eating, physical and social activities, sleep, physical care and well-being

- **Social withdrawal** and social difficulties

- **Fears** – sudden/unexpected

- **Developmentally inappropriate behaviours**, e.g. toileting accidents, thumb sucking, mouthing objects, baby talk, clinginess

- **Signs of sadness** – being unduly upset, crying easily

- **Signs of self-destructive behaviour**: head banging, excessive accidents (falls, dropping things and self-harm)

- **Morbid thoughts and talk**, for example about injury, death, illness and catastrophe.

What can parents do?

Parents need to be confident that their own expert knowledge of and long-term relationship with their particular child puts them in a central position for noticing and being aware of any major changes in their young person's social and physical function, daily routine and behaviour. Classic indicators of bullying are a young person being reluctant to go to school, unexplained bruises and/or marks, loss of or damage to possessions and missing lunch money and/or demands for more money for unexplained reasons.

In a possible bullying scenario all of the suggestions for good communication as described in Chapter 10 really come into play. This is a time when, if you can talk with your child in a non-judgemental manner, actively listen and understand what is happening and most importantly find out what they want to happen or not happen, you can make a big difference. The teenager who has reached the point of opening up to their parent/s needs reassurance that the bullying is not their fault, will be addressed and will not disadvantage them further. Sometimes a teenager will state that they do not want their parent to talk with the school but my experience in this situation is that unless the bullying is happening entirely out of school, this does have to happen. You can still reassure them that everything possible will be done to stop the bullying and to keep them safe at the same time, but because bullying can only thrive and continue where secrets and silences are maintained you have no choice. The other point to share with your teenager is that bullies very often have other victims, as their own reasons for bullying are rarely satisfied by picking on just one individual. In other words, the bully needs help to find a different way of behaving too. To help you go about involving the school as effectively as possible, keep a record of the details that you are aware of. If it is feasible then encourage your teenager to do the same. The more specific you can be about who is involved, the specific times, frequency and nature of the bullying and the effects, the easier it is for the school to put effective measures into place. These measures may well include whole-school work as part of their commitment to inclusion and social justice, a targeted anti-bullying social and emotional development project with a class or year group, and individual work with both victim and bully.

In the case of parents whose child is actually doing the bullying, the suggestions made above to parents of victims of bullying are similarly useful. It is essential to understand the young person's reasons for bullying and although it will not be an easy subject to talk about, parents have to gain some insight so that they can help. Bullying can never be condoned and this 'bottom line' must be made explicit, but this kind of behaviour, in my experience, only arises when there is something wrong in the bully's life and their unkind and harmful behaviour to their victim can sometimes be dangerous or even illegal with potentially serious repercussions for both victim and bully. Obviously no functional and healthy young person will engage in such risks and they need to talk with and to be helped by involved adults. I have met parents who did not want to address the fact that their young person was engaging in bullying behaviour because they were concerned about the possibility of punishment. However, if this can be viewed as a way of helping their child to get help to make changes, communicate and relate better, they can often accept and work constructively with the situation.

14. Intimate relationships and sexual development

Much that has already been covered in preceding chapters applies to this subject – the need for good communication, positive self-regard and the right combination of care and control from parents. During the middle- to late-teenage years, in tandem with the physical changes and overall progress to maturity, young people will begin to form romantic relationships, which by definition involve close physical intimacy, and investment of emotion, time and energy. They will spend a great deal of time thinking, fantasizing about and observing possible boyfriends and girlfriends. Many teenagers suffer agonies of self-doubt and worry about the prospect of being able to start such relationships, the implicit and necessary personal demands and the possibility of being rejected.

Teenagers' dating represents much more than the quest for a reproductive partner as it is a source of peer credibility and status and also another context in which their personal, social and emotional development can progress. In the UK and America the average teenage girl begins dating at least once a week from about fourteen years of age while the average teenage male does so a year or two later. The peer and social norms and stereotypes with which they are growing up influence both sexes. Most young people navigate the choppy waters of intimate relationships reasonably safely, but some do not as statistics on teenage pregnancies, terminations, sexually transmitted diseases and serious emotional issues reveal.

Organizations such as Brook* offer comprehensive, accessible and clear advice, information and training for schools on a whole range of topics relating to young people and intimate relationships and it is well worth both parents and teenagers looking at their website. Brook's key message is that many young people are unaware of the possible risks of sexual behaviour and intimate relationships, and of their rights to say no. They emphasize the importance of compulsory relationship and sex education in schools, and of the engagement of parents. For many years the UK Youth Parliament has been working to promote the idea of a 'Curriculum for Life', which includes relationship and sex education, and in 2018 Parliament approved of plans for compulsory relationship and sex education for all school-aged children. The fact that in Britain the rate of teenage pregnancies has been halved in the last two decades suggests that the public health and education policy must be working.

Teenage pregnancy

Cassie, aged fifteen, went to a school where relationship and sex education consisted of little more than an extra biology lesson for which the

---

* https://www.brook.org.uk

students were separated by sex. No timetabled lessons for teaching about personal relationships, sexual health and contraception took place. Most of Cassie's friends based their ideas on how to be women on commercialized celebrity role models and had unrealistic and highly romantic ideas about relationships with boys. Cassie's quest for her prince with whom she would find true love began in earnest when she started secretly meeting a man several years older, who worked in a garage on her route to school. She thought that in order to secure a long-term relationship with him she had to agree to sex, and trusted him when he said no contraception was necessary.

The 'less said about sexual matters the better' parental approach to Cassie's situation

In this scenario Cassie's parents took the view that their daughter should be protected from any discussion about sex or intimate relationships and restricted all possible interactions with boys. When Cassie started coming home late after school and her visits to friends at weekends increased markedly they became suspicious and started to meet her at the school gate and refuse permission for her to see friends. When she withdrew into herself and started to be sick in the mornings before school they were the last to realize what was happening and only found out when a particularly caring and observant teacher made contact.

The communicative and open parental approach to Cassie's situation in which sex is just one more subject for discussion

Cassie's parents have always talked with her in an open manner and no topics are considered off-limit, including sexual relationships. Often conversations would be triggered by television programmes, newspaper articles and films. When their daughter started to show an interest in romantic relationships they answered her questions about their own relationships with honesty, provided information about contraception and generally compensated for the absence of a good quality relationship and sex education programme at Cassie's school. In addition they made their home a welcoming place where she felt comfortable about bringing new friends, whom they got to know in a relaxed and down-to-earth manner, taking their lead from their daughter.

Sexuality

Will, aged sixteen, was a popular boy with many male and female friendships. He was an excellent footballer and had been scouted by a local professional team, so played every night after school and at weekends. He was perfectly happy until his two older brothers, both of whom had long-term girlfriends, began to tease him about the possibility that he was gay. Will had experimented sexually with one of his football friends and been very uncomfortable and deeply ashamed about the whole episode. He was becoming increasingly aware that most of the boys he knew were dating girls but he had no romantic or sexual feelings about girls and was becoming more and more unhappy and confused.

A traditional and prescriptive parental approach to Will's situation

Will's parents were very traditional in their approach to family life. His father and mother's relationship was highly gendered in that there were certain tasks and responsibilities that were considered to be a 'man's job' and others that were seen as 'women's work'. Will's mother took care of all things domestic and his father managed all DIY, money and car matters. When it came to their three sons they were expected to follow in their dad's footsteps – they were discouraged from learning how to cook, iron or do any kind of household tasks and encouraged to spend their leisure time watching sports or being with other young males. Humour was often of a sexist and/or homophobic nature and comments such as 'boys will be boys' and 'boys needing to sow their wild oats' were made on a daily basis. Relationships and feelings were not discussed and the only thing that Will and his brothers learnt about sex was that it was a male's right and natural instinct to want and have sex with as many females as he could before 'settling down' to married life. Will responded to this home atmosphere by becoming secretive about his personal life, cut off from his family and absent from home as much as possible. This added to his feelings of unhappiness, confusion and also to his vulnerability as he had few opportunities to share his concerns.

A more progressive and accepting parental approach to Will's situation

Will's parents had encouraged their three sons to talk with them and ask questions on any subject. They also encouraged their sons to do the same with each other, so when Will began to wonder about his sexuality he felt able to talk with his twenty-year-old brother and was reassured to be told that it was not unusual for young people of both sexes to have same-sex intimate relationships, usually, but not always, on a temporary basis, as part of the 'finding out about sex and themselves' phase of growing up. His brother told him of the need to take care of himself – to use condoms and to resist being coerced to have sex if he didn't want to. Will also talked to his brothers and his parents about the culture among his male friends of bragging about sexual conquests, and the pressure he was feeling at not wanting to be a sexual predator but wanting to continue to enjoy having girls as friends. At Will's school the PSHE programme was delivered to all pupils in a clear and down-to-earth manner and an emphasis placed upon relationships and sexual intimacy within these. Will learnt about the changing and more fluid trends and views on gender and of the fact that a continuum of sexual preferences and sexualities existed and that it was important for each individual to make the choices that were right for them, which made them feel fulfilled, safe, healthy and happy.

Pornography

Ollie first discovered pornography in her parents' bedroom when she was about eight years of age. She was so worried by what she had seen that she became withdrawn and much less sociable, thinking that this was the only way to manage her own sexual development and, in her mind, her increasing vulnerability. She was also deeply worried about the fact that she was growing pubic hair, had a different and bigger body, but smaller breasts, than any of the porn stars she had viewed, and so felt unacceptable and abnormal. By the time she was thirteen she was increasingly reluctant to speak to boys, wore clothes that covered her up as much as possible, spent more and more time alone writing poems and stories and keeping a diary and developed an eating disorder where she either binged on sweets and high-calorie snacks or tried to eat very little indeed.

A parental approach to Ollie's situation prioritizing appearance

Ollie's parents had always placed great store upon physical appearance. Her parents both spent a lot of time and money on their own wardrobes and physical fitness and were non-plussed by the fact that their daughter didn't seem to care about how she looked. Her father in particular only seemed to be able to notice his daughter in terms of her outward appearance and was unaware of her interests and progress at school, which was actually quite good. Her mother constantly encouraged Ollie to join her on her latest diet or exercise regime, but as her ideas were rejected began to just leave her to her own devices, hoping that she would grow out of 'this ugly duckling phase'. In terms of Ollie's sexual development, neither of her parents ever talked about the subject and assumed that would be covered by her school. Ollie became increasingly obsessed with eating as little as possible, comparing herself in a negative manner to other girls and women. She spent as much time as she could on her own and her range of interests and social connections dwindled.

A parental approach to Ollie's situation that values the whole person

Ollie's parents made a conscious effort to encourage their daughter's interests and took great pleasure in her academic achievements and love of books and writing. They were aware of the unhelpful stereotypes regarding women's appearance and often had everyday conversations about the range and diversity of female and male physical attractiveness along with other personal qualities, such as a sense of humour, enthusiasm, creativity, sociability and kindness. These conversations were often prompted by watching television and films with their daughter or by books or newspaper articles that they and she found interesting. In terms of exercise and diet they spoke of these in terms of healthy lifestyles and about the personal benefits rather than the emphasis being upon being physically attractive to the opposite sex. They would plan and prepare food as a family and provided good, well-balanced role models of eating and enjoying food. They took an interest in Ollie's school PSHE programme and were aware of subjects being covered so that they could talk in a natural way about their own growing-up and relationships and also be available for any questions Ollie might have. Ollie was able to bring up the subject of pornography and this gave her parents the chance to share their views that pornography had little to do with intimate relationships, which involved emotional and full engagement with another person, was an aspect of some adults' fantasy lives and was generally unreal, sometimes violent and all about making money for those involved in producing it. As a result of Ollie's conversations with her parents she started to become more sociable, to feel more content with her appearance and to develop a more balanced attitude to eating, exercise and lifestyle in general.

Consider some other issue to do with intimate relationships and sexual development, for example, what happens when an intimate relationship ends, when an ex-boyfriend or

-girlfriend becomes vindictive and spreads rumours or engages in online attacks, or when a teenager becomes involved in an abusive relationship. There are many more possibilities but choose one that is concerning you and consider possible ways of dealing with that issue and situation. You may wish to do this on your own, with another adult and/or even with your teenager. When you have done so, consider the points in the acronym below, which summarizes some suggestions for parents helping their teenagers with issues surrounding intimacy.

Impulsive, emotional and unreasoned behaviour are usually evident when a teenager is 'in love', especially for the first time. Teenagers, like most people, are likely to be affected by the complex processes of their 'emotional brain' – the limbic system – in early intimate relationships where, by definition, people are at their most vulnerable and exposed. Unlike adults, however, the reasoned and rational behaviour, which is increasingly evident as a result of the mature frontal cortex, is not consistently available to young people

Never lecture but listen, reassure and be honest, when asked, about your own learning from and about relationships

Talk about intimacy and sexual development should be natural and part of everyday conversations and may use the stereotypes on TV etc. as starting points for discussion. You can use this material as well as your teenager's comments as prompts and it will be more 'teenager led'

Intimacy and sexual acts and/or behaviour between adults and teenagers is never acceptable and hopefully your son or daughter's earlier education, at home and school about saying no, personal space and staying safe, will have been such that they are clear about this. If they don't seem to be, parents should feel confident to have conversations that remind them

Measured, timely, matter-of-fact and unrushed responses to a teenager's questions on and worries about intimacy and sexual development are best

Awareness of your particular young person's overall well-being and behaviour should always be an ongoing priority for parents, so that if necessary professional support is sought where there is cause for serious concern. (See the checklist on page 161 for warning signs to look out for)

Choice, self-respect and reciprocity are key to intimate relationships, so teenagers should be encouraged to understand that making these choices should never be done when they are drunk or under the influence of drugs and therefore unable to make clear self-protective choices

Young people benefit from information that is reasonably simple, not too soon, not too late, down to earth and practical.

15. Teenagers' learning

Child development specialists such as Jean Piaget (see my book *A Practical Guide to Child Psychology*, details in references) have demonstrated through their research that children are born with a natural desire to learn, to problem-solve and to engage in exploratory behaviour. Teachers have to use these innate drives in order to teach the curriculum. As children enter the teenage years the curriculum demands increase, formal examinations loom and they are hopefully developing aspirations for future employment and higher-level studies and training. As well as all these factors they need to become more independent, more self-organized and increasingly self-propelling in their studies.

Much of my work as an educational psychologist has involved issues to do with learning. This is a big area and as for all aspects of my practice requires consideration and enquiry into a number of areas. For example, all individuals have their preferred and most effective learning styles; need to understand how they learn best – develop good metacognition skills and self-awareness; and ideally can access the school curriculum in a way that suits them best.

Different learning styles

Teachers, more than anyone, are aware of the fact that every student has their own unique profile of learning abilities and preferred learning style(s), which become(s) more apparent as they mature. In the 1980s two British researchers, Honey and Mumford (see references), built upon the work of an earlier theorist, Kolb, and produced their own learning styles questionnaire and this took the British education system by storm. They proposed that there were four different types of learners:

- **Activists**: Individuals who learn by doing. The learning activities can be brainstorming, problem-solving, group discussion, puzzles, competitions or role-play etc.

- **Theorists**: These learners like to understand the ideas/concepts behind the activities. Their choice of learning activities includes models, statistics, stories, quotes, background information, applying concepts theoretically etc.

- **Pragmatists**: These individuals are able to see how to put the learning into practice in their present situation. They learn better through taking time to think about how to apply learning in reality, looking at case studies, problem-solving and discussion

- **Reflectors**: These individuals learn by watching and thinking about events and happenings. They like paired discussions, self-analysis questionnaires, personality questionnaires, time out, observing activities, feedback from others, coaching, interviews etc.

Rather than thinking of yourself and your teenager as having just one learning style, consider each style, and rate yourself and your teenager, ideally with them, on a scale of one to ten, on how much you associate with each style. One means that style is hardly evident in your learning and ten means it is extremely evident.

What do you notice, which styles are most evident? Which styles might be cultivated and do you have ideas for how this might be done?

When Honey and Mumford's questionnaire was published, some very simplistic ideas about the idea of how individuals learnt gained currency and are still prevalent despite criticisms of over-simplification and generalization. I've heard people talking about 'visual', 'kinaesthetic', 'auditory', 'social' etc. learners on many occasions, as though these labels were sufficient for describing a young person's entire approach to learning, and a theoretical but not realistic or practical segregation of modes for learning. I always take care to acknowledge an individual's seeming preferences but also gently suggest ways of drawing upon and linking in with other modes as the successful and effective learner needs to do this as much as possible. An ideal learning environment generally offers a multi-sensory learning experience as much as possible. This is probably why the use of new technology is so popular and accessible to most students, including those with particular and additional (relative to their peers) learning needs.

Although the concept of learning styles has been discredited to some degree and teachers are not administering the learning styles questionnaire or later derivatives of this to anywhere near the same degree as was the case previously, nevertheless, some useful ideas do remain. Here's a summary that will be useful to bear in mind as you try to support your own teenager's learning.

Prior to Honey and Mumford's work most people did not tend to reflect upon how they learnt, but the ideas of Honey and Mumford:

1. Enabled a better understanding of what might help individual's learning and this in turn was useful in deciding the best options for study, i.e. choice of subjects and courses, ways of studying or in addressing difficulties with learning.

2. Helped teachers and educationalists offer and extend a wider range of learning experiences, e.g. varying and combining formal, informal, planned and impromptu learning/teaching activities.

3. Ensured a better understanding of individual learning styles, strengths and weaknesses, and enabled the development of metacognition (learning how to learn) strategies.

Metacognition and independent study skills

Metacognition
- Higher order thinking
- Thinking about one's own learning processes and approaches
- A means to increasing and enabling understanding, analysis and control of one's cognitive processes
- Particularly evident and helpful when engaged in learning.

As an educational psychologist I often frame the processes of learning in terms of information input, processing, organizing and application. I try to encourage adults involved over time – teachers and family – in supporting young people's learning to help them to be aware of and understand why they find some things easy to learn and some things more difficult. The information from my in-depth assessments is used to help with this process and sharing this with the young people in an accessible and applicable matter is important. Teachers obviously have to manage many students at group, class, year group and even whole school levels, but at the same time have to be aware of individual students' needs and to meet these as closely as possible. Apart from the curriculum delivery and actual teaching, they are involved in supporting the complex psychological processes involved in young people's learning and development. This includes:

- Ensuring emotional support, including encouragement and setting realistic, positive expectations
- Offering reassurance and practical solutions
- Appropriately staged and timed learning experiences
- Providing accessible and engaging materials
- Giving feedback on progress, attitude, effort and outcomes, ideally involving the teenager as much as possible, encouraging them to be active in monitoring and evaluating their own learning.

Parents generally recognize when their teenager is experiencing the above because the teachers who offer this quality of learning experience are usually their favourites. Such teachers are worth making a connection with and can be a mine of information on how to help your particular teenager's school learning.

One last point is that of encouraging you not to do so much and to be so involved with your teenager's studies that an unhelpful dependency is set up. Martin Seligman, best known for his social learning theory and research, first coined the phrase 'learned helplessness', which is a phenomenon in which a person becomes so conditioned to being helped by another that they lose all sense of their own capacity to help themselves. Clearly one of the most important skills that parents and education professionals want to ensure is that young people have a sense of being able to help themselves and draw upon their own skills and capacities.

Here's another helpful acronym, providing ideas for parents to support the development of metacognition and independent study skills:

Have positive and regular communication with your teenager's school ...

Especially teachers with whom your teenager enjoys a good relationship – if you don't know who then ask your son or daughter

Let your teenager know about your own learning experiences – positive and less so – and tell them what helped; keep the focus of such revelations ...

Positive and realistic as this feedback is necessary in relation to the young person's capacity to learn and their actual achievements

Initiate conversations about the fact that everyone has strengths and weaknesses, favourite subjects, lessons and teachers

Not so favourite subjects, teachers and lessons are also good to talk about as long as you can emphasize learning opportunities that can be ...

Gained and used as ways of material for growth and improved learning

Letting teenagers make choices about their learning always entails the possibility that they will make mistakes and even experience failure

Explain what your choices would be and why, but don't try to force your teenager to emulate you

Action plans, targets, timetables and timescales are useful, especially if the teenager has created them, but try to encourage them to be …

Realistic and feasible, through interested, unpressured conversations with lots of open questions

Not all subject areas lend themselves to the same methods of studies. Have conversations about different ways of tackling the different demands, e.g. learning strategies research, reading widely in different formats, writing information out, repetition, discussion and practical activities

ICT is now an intrinsic part of most teenagers' learning landscape, so consider what you can reasonably supply and make available

Notice when they are particularly pleased with an achievement and/or aspect of their schoolwork and encourage celebration

Groups and partners for tackling homework and study sessions often appeal to most inherently sociable teenagers, so help to support this. On the other hand, if they need a silent, interruption-free space try to arrange this in discussion with them too.

Learning issues?

As I've emphasized throughout this book, its focus is upon 'normal' teenage behaviour, i.e. not upon the range of behaviours associated with clinical disorders and what is sometimes termed 'abnormal psychology', which includes the wide range of learning difficulties and disorders, often referred to as special educational needs (SENs). Students with SENs always have significantly more difficulties with learning and/or development, relative to what would usually be expected of other students of their age or, in the case of students with specific learning difficulties such as dyslexia, relative to what would be expected of their literacy development and performance, taking into account their overall academic performance and learning opportunities. Where the possibility of SENs exists it is important that an assessment takes place. This usually gets picked up long before the teenage years, but not always. For many students the assessment will take place in school by school staff, but sometimes other professionals need to be involved, for example, an educational psychologist, medical professional or speech and language or occupational therapist.

One of the most useful books that tackles students' learning issues that I've come across and often recommend to parents is *Smart but Scattered*, written by American psychologists Peg Dawson and Richard Guare. It draws upon ideas from neuropsychology and educational and clinical psychology and it is actually relevant to adults too in many respects. It claims to be able to help parents and their children with a wide range of common difficulties to do with executive skills – those aspects of the brain's higher order processing activities such as:

- Organization
- Impulse control
- Focus and attention
- Time management
- Planning
- Follow-through and task completion
- Learning from mistakes
- Emotional control
- Independent problem-solving
- Resourcefulness.

All of the above are necessary skills and characteristics for successful learning and overall development, but they take time, practice and persistence to develop. In an ideal world adult role models such as parents would be able to demonstrate these but in truth, most people's overall executive development is a 'work in progress'.

One of the key ideas in this book is that the experience of parenting teenagers is a huge growth and learning opportunity in itself for the adults involved, so the next activity is for parents to do in relation to themselves and to then apply the ideas that come from this to their teenager's learning issues.

Dawson and Guare use a method of clarifying, understanding and addressing issues that draws heavily upon behaviourist theory (see Chapter 4). The key points to their method are summed up in the ABC approach:

Antecedents – address/change the environment in which the issue is evident

Behaviour – address the behaviour – teach/develop the necessary skill

Consequence – change the consequence through reward or incentives.

First, choose an area of executive skill that you would like to target and improve – a skill that would make a good improvement to an aspect of family life, usually a routine aspect. Then complete the following table:

The issue:

A	Current situation?	How could the environment be changed?
B	What behaviour is happening?	What behaviour/skill needs to develop?
C	What happens as a result?	What consequence/incentive can be introduced?

Here is a worked example of a common issue:

The issue: planning family meals

A	Current situation?	How could the environment be changed?
	• Often the fridge is empty or too much food is prepared and then thrown away.	• A chalk board to be kept on the fridge with columns for meals on each day of the week, which everyone can initial if they want to eat and an empty column for weekends where everyone in the family has to put their initials if they want to eat and/or cook. • A shopping list and pen to be kept on the kitchen top to note down shopping items needed, which everyone should add to as required.
B	What behaviour is happening?	What behaviour/skill needs to develop?
	• Meals for which you are largely responsible are very ad hoc. • Food quantity, quality and variety rarely satisfactory.	• Thinking about the week ahead – Mon to Fri. • Matching food needs with supply. • Communicating the above as a family.
C	What happens as a result?	What consequence/incentive can be introduced?
	• Lots of snack-based and low-quality meals 'on the run', missed meals or expensive takeaways and meals out. • Lots of moaning and bad temper regarding the above.	• More family meal time where everyone is eating well. • Less expensive, more money available. • More paced, appropriately equipped and enjoyable meal preparation.

If you can manage to follow through on the above you are likely to see the benefits not just for yourself, but for the family as a whole, but it will probably take time and persistence. Talk about what you are doing to the other family members, especially the teenager(s), and when you do experience benefits talk about these even more. In doing so you are providing an excellent and proactive model of behaviour, an openness to learn and change and owning up to the fact that there is always room for improvement. The systematic approach is a great aid to most practical aspects of living and to studying and if your teenager observes the benefits, even becomes involved and contributes, you can be sure that they are learning an important way of living life as an adult.

---

16. Lifestyle choices – drink, drugs, gambling, exercise and diet

As I've written throughout this book, a key drive for teenagers is that of having as much choice in and control of their lives as possible. This increases as they age, which is unsurprising as in many respects this appetite for free will and control in one's own life is the hallmark of being an adult. However, teenagers are by nature more impulsive, more inclined to take risks, more emotionally expressive and less aware of the repercussions of their actions than grown-ups, because of their stage of development. Cognitive neuroscientist Sarah-Jayne Blakemore (see references) speaks about the effects of the developing prefrontal cortex in adolescents and its observable effects on teenagers' behaviour and choices resulting from the development of higher order cognitive processes such as decision making, planning, impulse control, social interaction and awareness. Parents have to achieve a balance of care and control in order to support their children's development and to ensure their safety.

A healthy and functional teenager is striving for choice and control and when they do so this is a testament to their successful growth and development and should be a cause for celebration. However, as parents know, it very often isn't and can be a primary source of conflict and unhappiness.

This chapter looks at some aspects of teen lifestyle that can cause parents concern, get a lot of largely negative and extreme coverage in the media and can sometimes seriously threaten a teenager's health, achievement, socialization, well-being and safety.

THINK ABOUT IT Think back to your own teenage years and recall the choices, behaviours and attitudes about which you now, as a more experienced and perhaps, but not necessarily, better-informed adult, would be concerned. Imagine what you would say to the teenager you once were and also think about what you would have liked from your parents at that time. The detail isn't necessarily going to be the same for your own teenage son or daughter, but the underlying themes of control/choice, belonging and achievement will be.

Alcohol and drugs

Alcohol and drugs are a feature of contemporary life, so understandably teenagers are going to want to find out about their effects and most will experiment but will not go on to develop a dependency. Schools can and do help the situation by providing accurate information about the dangers, ensuring a quality of communication in which teenagers can ask questions and express worries, and also offer suggestions for reducing the risks. In my clinical experience the teenagers who manage this aspect of the social world have parents who:

1. Are honest and open about their own experiences and learning.

2. Demonstrate through example moderate and safe alcohol use.

3. Are informed and up to date about drugs through their own research and also their familiarity with their children's school PSHE programme and on this basis provide factual information to their teenagers through lots of everyday, relaxed and matter-of-fact conversations over time.

4. Set and maintain clear boundaries such as a zero tolerance of any illegal substances in the home.

5. Are in tune with their teenager's behaviour, general health and moods so that they notice any significant changes as soon as possible (see page 161 for warning signs to look out for) and access additional support as necessary.

Take any of your thoughts about the points 1 to 5 above, and write a letter to your teenager starting with:

Dear ....,

I know that if you haven't already done so you are going to meet or hear about or even see people who take drugs or drink large amounts of alcohol because that is the world we live in. ....

....

....

....

....

....

You might use this exercise as a way of starting some new conversations with your teenager; you may even show them the letter.

Gambling and credit

Money equates to power in our society and the quest to have as much as possible, especially without having to work particularly hard, is a fantasy that is very much abroad these days. Once someone reaches adulthood then it is very much up to them how they earn, use and manage their financial assets, but plenty of adults have life-long problems in relation to this. Schools are gradually including more practical advice and information on this subject into their teaching, partly because of the increasing problems of gambling, living on credit and the heightened awareness of the strong correlations between poverty and health and well-being, but also because young people themselves are voicing the need for help with this important life skill. Schools in England were required for the first time in 2013/14 to teach students about managing their money, financial products and public finances. The national curriculum now includes financial education within mathematics and citizenship lessons. This is a recognition of the importance of young people having the skills and knowledge to make sound financial decisions and hopefully avoid some of the many dangers. However, there is no explicit mention of gambling and given the prevalence of this both online and in many gambling outlets, and its appeal to young people, there is still much to do, and in the meantime parents have to do their best to help their teenagers be informed and make wise choices. A search online for financial education resources may be a good exercise and could trigger some useful conversations. As I emphasize in the acronym below, it is a good idea to share your own best tips for everyday budgeting and money management.

The following acronym offers some ideas for what parents can do to help their teenagers manage money:

Managing money is always going to boil down to the simple equation: 'money in should equal or be more than money out'

Openness and honesty about how much money is available and about how much is needed can be modelled by parents to their teenagers. It is never too early to start conversations about this subject and as the young person's personal budget increases, to actually show how it can be organized and managed

Needs, actual and perceived, are not necessarily the same and frequently not necessities, so again, lots of conversations on this subject from a young age will help teenagers be aware of the choices they do and can make

Examples set by parents regarding how money is managed and the financial decision-making processes involved have a great influence on their children's attitudes and behaviour

Your priorities in relation to money will be evident, whether or not you talk openly about them. If you have a strong and helpful saving habit, use credit and spend before the money is earned, or work more in order to earn more you can be sure your teenager will take note and that this will influence their money-related choices.

Exercise and diet

It's common sense that in order to have a healthy body a healthy lifestyle is needed – the right blend of exercise, wholesome food and sufficient hydration. Teenagers often stretch their days or even begin to blur days and nights and can be so enthusiastically involved in their interests and social lives that they literally forget to eat and drink sufficiently. This is where the wise and in-tune parent can provide prompts and reminders but does not fall into the nagging trap. There is some good advice online (see references), which will help you, and if you notice that your teenager's exercise and/or eating has become markedly erratic and/or insufficient or particularly unhealthy, try to take this approach but also keep an eye on the situation (see warnings checklist, page 161), talk to other involved adults and get help if you have concerns. Obtaining professional support, even if only at an advisory level, is best done as early as possible.

You cannot force a teenager to become more or less physically active, to eat more healthily, regularly and appropriately, but you can provide the framework of support and interest, example, appetizing meals and food and even try to cook together, but be prepared to let the teenager lead and/or manage the process as soon as they have the basic skills and knowledge. I've noticed that so many adults regret not having the necessary cooking and nutrition skills once they're living independently and have often heard the view expressed that the kitchen was their parents' domain.

Start by talking about your teenager's favourite cooked foods with them and finding out what they would like to be able to make for themselves. Make a point of having all the ingredients and also the time to take them through what is involved. You may need to do this more than once but when you consider they have the necessary skills and knowledge and are safe to follow the recipe independently, arrange it so that they can do so with you very much in the background or even in another room. Be prepared for less than perfect end results and a messier kitchen than usual but remember that over time, with your support and encouragement, there will be benefits to everyone in the family. You will find this works best if you can manage to make the cooking sessions fairly spontaneous.

17. Difficult feelings

Every adult remembers the emotionally difficult times of the intense period of development they faced as a teenager and much of the content of preceding chapters involves teenagers and their difficult feelings at different times. Issues to do with self-esteem; specific or generalized sadness, stress, worries and insecurities; making mistakes; experiencing social challenges such as finding and making friends, boyfriends and girlfriends; difficulties and choices to do with studies, work and lifestyle can accumulate to the point that the young person feels overwhelmed and as a parent you can be at a loss as to know what to do or say. These days, on top of all this, according to the Department of Health in the UK, currently one in four teenagers will experience mental health issues and popular media is active in broadcasting material related to this, while at the same time reporting daily the dangers that teenagers face in the modern world and the consequent mishaps. However, the degree of emotional challenge varies enormously, with some young people seeming to breeze through without problems and the large majority experiencing only some problems some of the time, and then there are those whose problems mean that they fit the criteria for clinical conditions such as depression, anxiety, eating disorders etc. If there is any concern that your teenager may be suffering from one of these conditions, the checklist on page 161 will highlight the areas affected and this should be shared as soon as possible with the family's GP or possibly another professional from health, education or social services.

This book is unashamedly solution focused in approach and underlying outlook because it has been my experience through many years of clinical practice as an applied psychologist, as a teacher and as a parent that this is the most likely way of addressing difficulties, bringing about positive change and most importantly of having hope to do so. When we consider the subject of teenagers' difficult feelings, it is useful to also consider the times and situations when their feelings are relatively easy, in other words the happier times.

Research into teenagers' well-being and happiness has found that the factors that most contribute to these are:

- Individual disposition
- The context, social and environmental
- Parental positivity and encouragement as embodied in their words *and* actions.

The focus of this book is upon the average and non-clinical population of teenagers and there is a lot that can be done, both by parents and by teenagers themselves, to cope with difficult feelings and to be happier. The most successful clinical interventions for young people who are experiencing difficult feelings include:

- Ensuring a healthy lifestyle, i.e. sleep, eating, exercise, social activities and personal space
- A balanced approach to the use of new technology and a varied diet of age-appropriate media experiences
- A range of activities and interests including those of a physical and social nature
- Positive and balanced adult role models
- Families in which communication is inclusive, open, regular and frequent.

There are no quick fixes to the complex issue of difficult feelings but it is important that the young person is reassured that when they feel like this it is not a matter of something being wrong with them, but that it is an indication that some changes need to be made, and that their parents are there for them. I also recommend that parents try to wait until the request is made by their son or daughter. One of the most unhelpful conversation starters with teenagers, in my experience, is 'how are you feeling?' A direct request to talk about emotions can be experienced as intrusive and overly intense. It is necessary, on the whole, to trust in your teenager to open up to you in their own time and own way. The following quote from a teenage girl expresses some of the reasons for this:

> *Please don't ask me how I'm feeling because I don't understand either.*
>
> Anonymous

I have been cautious throughout this book in suggesting that you don't necessarily do the practical exercises with your teenager straight away and to generally do them with yourself first instead, so that you can then introduce natural and low-key conversations around the new thoughts you have had.

In my book on child psychology (see references), I have written about some therapeutic approaches that are particularly useful for supporting young people, including cognitive behavioural therapy (CBT) and solution-focused brief therapy. I would also add mindfulness, active relaxation, positive affirmation and visualization, but it is best for parents to read up on these before suggesting their son or daughter participate in exercises about which they have learnt. For example, the Centre for Child Mental Health produces some excellent publications for parents and their website is worth looking at (see references for this and other sources), for example the page entitled 'Draw on Your Emotions', in which it explains how through drawing the young person can express how they are feeling and what may help.

18. Conclusion – final thoughts

As I wrote from the very first chapter, I have drawn heavily upon positive psychology throughout this book and this involves a focus upon the strengths and virtues of any situation and/or issue(s) and then actively using these to create and implement solutions. When we consider teenagers the common and rather negative belief is that they're difficult and a big challenge. The media thrives on amplifying such a viewpoint so hopefully this book may change things a little and certainly give more hope as well as some practical strategies. I've been talking to many people: parents and relatives; professionals in health, education, the law and social services; young people themselves; children who will one day be teenagers and lots of others for years, and I always try to find out about their views on the positive aspects of teenagers. Here are some of the points they have made:

- Humour and a sense of fun
- Energy and enthusiasm
- Sociability and an enjoyment in doing things with others
- Commitment, determination and application to what they believe is important
- Passion and deep beliefs
- Adventurousness and a love of the new and novel
- Hope and anticipation; a focus on the future

- Loyalty and trust in family and friends and being trustworthy
- Confidence in succeeding
- Creativity and different thinking
- Empathy, compassion and caring for others and their feelings
- Flexibility and a willingness to adapt.

 THINK ABOUT IT Look at the list above and note which qualities apply to your teenager and when. Think about the factors and circumstances that make these most apparent.

Nearly all of the parents with whom I have worked love their teenagers to the point that they would do and/or sacrifice most things to help them move effectively and appropriately into adulthood safely. Not only do they have to decide and enforce rules and regulations but they also have to offer emotional, practical and financial support. They have to provide the right information at the right time and carry a multitude of different roles. It is hardly surprising that having teenagers can feel burdensome and that nearly all parents, at some point, wonder if they're up to the endless demands and expectations. As well as all this most parents' memories of the dramas of their own teenage years are all too vivid and many consider that their own parents didn't do or give them what they needed. I think this seemingly universal mismatch between expectations and the reality of parenting teenagers is necessary as it ensures we are always striving to do better. It's also inevitable because our children are growing up into a different world to the one that we and the generations before us did. What is important to hold on to is the undeniable fact that the majority of people live their lives in the hope that their parents will be proud of them and I know from direct experience that when parents pass on, this realization becomes particularly clear.

Kahlil Gibran, Lebanese-American writer, poet and visual artist, wrote:

You are the bows from which your children
as living arrows are sent forth.

This quote reminds me of the undeniable fact that we can learn from our teenagers and that our own personal development can benefit. The challenges that each unique teenager is almost certainly going to present means we have to dig deep into our own reserves of positivity, realism, energy, creativity, empathy, acceptance, congruence, humour and optimism, and above all else, we have to keep talking. I hope very much that this book will be of some help in that process.

References

Online articles

Sarah-Jayne Blakemore's TED Talk on the mysterious workings of the adolescent brain (2012): https://www.ted.com/talks/sarah_jayne_blakemore_the_mysterious_workings_of_the_adolescent_brain

Department for Education (UK) (2005) 'Social and Emotional Aspects of Learning': http://webarchive.nationalarchives.gov.uk/20110812101121/http://nsonline.org.uk/node/87009

U.S. National Library of Medicine (2017) 'Adolescent Development': https://medlineplus.gov/ency/article/002003.htm

Stanford Children's Health, 'The Growing Child': http://www.stanfordchildrens.org/en/topic/default?id=the-growing-child-adolescent-13-to-18-years-90-P02175

NHS, 'Healthy Eating for Teens': https://www.nhs.uk/live-well/eat-well/healthy-eating-for-teens/

Office for National Statistics (UK), 2017 National census information on demographical information regarding families: https://www.ons.gov.uk/peoplepopulationandcommunity/birthsdeathsandmarriages/families/bulletins/familiesandhouseholds/2017

SafeTeens, 'Nutrition & Exercise': http://www.safeteens.org/nutrition-exercise/

Hardey, M. & Atkinson, R. (2018) 'Disconnected: Non-users of Information Communication Technologies', *Sociological Research Online*: http://dro.dur.ac.uk/24154/

BBC 4, 'Thinking Allowed': https://www.bbc.co.uk/programmes/b006qy05 – This series has many episodes pertinent to teenage development and issues

Schrum, Kelly (2004) *Some Wore Bobby Sox: The Emergence of Teenage Girls' Culture, 1920–1945*, New York: Palgrave Macmillan. Available online: https://onlinelibrary.wiley.com/doi/abs/10.1111/j.1748-5959.2008.00152.x

Peterson, Christopher (2008) 'What Is Positive Psychology and What Is It Not?', psychologytoday.com: https://www.psychologytoday.com/gb/blog/the-good-life/200805/what-is-positive-psychology-and-what-is-it-not – This is a blog post associated with the popular psychology magazine *Psychology Today*

Books

Austin, Joe & Willard, Michael Nevin (1998) *Generations of Youth: Youth Cultures and History in Twentieth-Century America*, New York: New York University Press

Bainbridge, David (2010) *Teenagers: A Natural History*, London: Portobello Books

Burnham, John (1986) *Family Therapy*, Abingdon: Routledge

Cullen, Kairen (2018) *A Practical Guide to Child Psychology: Understand Your Kids and Enjoy Parenting*, London: Icon Books

Dawson, P. & Guare, R. (2008) *Smart but Scattered: The revolutionary 'executive skills' approach to helping kids reach their potential*, London: Guildford Press – Good strategies for supporting the learning and development of young people and adults alike

Faber, A. & Mazlish, E. (2006) *How to Talk So Teens Will Listen & Listen So Teens Will Talk*, London: Piccadilly Press

Fenwick, E. & Smith, T. (1993) *Adolescence – The Survival Guide for Parents and Teenagers*, London: Dorling Kindersley

Gordon, J. & Grant, G. (1997) *How We Feel – An Insight into the Emotional World of Teenagers*, London: Jessica Kingsley Publishers

Honey, P. & Mumford, A. (1986) *The Manual of Learning Styles*, London: Peter Honey Publications

Huppert, F.A. (2009) 'Psychological Well-being: Evidence Regarding Its Causes and Consequences', Review commissioned by the UK government for the Foresight Mental Capital and Wellbeing Project (http://www.foresight.gov.uk/index.asp)

Jensen, E. & Snider, C. (2013) *Turnaround Tools for the Teenage Brain – Helping Underperforming Students Become Lifelong Learners*, San Francisco: Jossey Bass

Kolb, D.A. (1984) *Experiential Learning*, Upper Saddle River, NJ: Prentice Hall

Nicolson, Doula and Ayers, Harry (2004) *Adolescent Problems*, London: David Fulton

Palladino, Grace (1996) *Teenagers: An American History*, Basic: New York

Piper, Katie with Piper, Diane (2018) *From Mother to Daughter: The Things I'd Tell My Child*, London: Quercus

Reingold Gluck, B. & Rosenfeld, J. (2005) *How to Survive Your Teenager*, Georgia: Hundreds of Head Books, Inc.

Roffey, S., Tarrant, T. & Majors, K. (1994) *Young Friends; Schools and Friendship*, London: Cassell

Satir, Virginia (1976) *Making Contact*, USA: Celestial Arts

Satir, Virginia (1988) *The New Peoplemaking*, Palo Alto, CA: Science and Behavior Books, Inc.

Snowling, M.J., Muter, V. & Carroll, J.M. (2007) 'Children at family risk of dyslexia: A follow-up in adolescence', *Journal of Child Psychology and Psychiatry*, 48, 609–618

Stern, Julian (2017) *Can I Tell You about Loneliness?*, London: Jessica Kingsley Publishers Ltd – This is one of many helpful titles in the 'Can I Tell You about …' series

Strasburger, V.C., Wilson, B.J. & Jordan, A.B. (Eds) (2009) *Children, Adolescents and the Media* (2nd edition), London: Sage

Umeh, K. (2009) *Understanding Adolescent Health Behaviour – A Decision Making Perspective*, Cambridge: Cambridge University Press

Varma, Ved (Ed.) (1997) *Troubles of Children and Adolescents*, London: Jessica Kingsley Publishers Ltd.

Helpful organizations

American Psychological Association: www.apa.org/

Association of Young People's Health (AYPH) (UK): http://www.youngpeopleshealth.org.uk/ – An organization researching young people's health, working with professionals and contributing to local and national strategy

Australian Psychological Society: www.psychology.org.au/

British Association for Behavioural and Cognitive Psychotherapy: www.babcp.com/

British Psychological Society: www.bps.org.uk/

Centre for Child Mental Health (UK): https://www.childmental healthcentre.org

Child Law Advice (UK): https://childlawadvice.org.uk – Operated by Coram Children's Legal Centre, they provide specialist advice and information on child, family and education law to parents, carers and young people in England

Childhelp (US): www.childhelp.org – Online helpline for children and young people

Childline (UK): www.childline.org.uk – Online helpline for children and young people

European Federation of Psychologists' Associations: www.efpa.eu/

International Association for Applied Psychology: https://iaapsy.org

International Society for Child and Play Therapy: www.playtherapy.org/

Mind (UK): www.mind.org.uk

National Children's Bureau (UK): www.ncb.org.uk/

National Society for the Prevention of Cruelty to Children (NSPCC) (UK): https://www.nspcc.org.uk

Parents Anonymous (US): parentsanonymous.org – Parenting training, support groups and helpline

Psychological Society of South Africa: www.psyssa.com/

UNICEF: www.unicef.org – Includes information on human rights for children and young people

The information above, largely relevant to the UK and the US, is available globally online, but country-specific organizations such as government departments for health, education and children and young people; psychological associations; and parent and teenager helplines can be found through searching online.

Index

Notes

Notes

Other titles in
the Practical Guides series

A Practical Guide to Building Self-Esteem

ISBN: 9781785783913
eISBN: 9781848313668

A Practical Guide to Child Psychology

ISBN: 9781785783227
eISBN: 9781848313293

A Practical Guide to Counselling

ISBN: 9781785783821
eISBN: 9781848316287

A Practical Guide to Emotional Intelligence

ISBN: 9781785783234
eISBN: 9781848314382

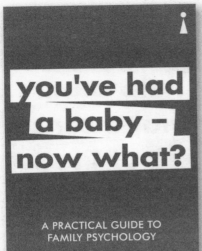

**A Practical Guide to
Family Psychology**

ISBN: 9781785784729
eISBN: 9781848315365

**A Practical Guide to
Mindfulness**

ISBN: 9781785783838
eISBN: 9781848313750